For my mother

ACKNOWLEDGMENTS

This book would not have been possible without the support, guidance and encouragement of my husband and best friend, Andrew Tompkins.

Special thanks also to Enara, Sean and Aaron, who have taught me more about autism and being a parent than any university ever could.

Finally, thank you to all the wonderful families who were willing to share their stories, so that others could benefit from their experiences.

TALKING WITH YOUR CHILD ABOUT THEIR AUTISM DIAGNOSIS

A guide for parents

Raelene Dundon

Jessica Kingsley *Publishers*
London and Philadelphia

First published in 2018
by Jessica Kingsley Publishers
73 Collier Street
London N1 9BE, UK
and
400 Market Street, Suite 400
Philadelphia, PA 19106, USA

www.jkp.com

Library of Congress Cataloging in Publication Data
Names: Dundon, Raelene, author.
Title: Talking with your child about their autism diagnosis : a guide for
    parents / Raelene Dundon.
Description: London ; Philadelphia : Jessica Kingsley Publishers, 2017. |
    Includes bibliographical references.
Identifiers: LCCN 2017021591 | ISBN 9781785922770 (alk. paper)
Subjects: LCSH: Autism in children. | Parents of autistic children. |
    Autistic children--Care. | Communication.
Classification: LCC RJ506.A9 D86 2017 | DDC 618.92/85882--
dc23 LC record available at https://lccn.loc.gov/2017021591

British Library Cataloguing in Publication Data
A CIP catalogue record for this book is available from the British Library

ISBN 978 1 78592 277 0
eISBN 978 1 78450 577 6

Printed and bound in Great Britain

MIX
Paper from
responsible sources
FSC® C013056

CONTENTS

PART 1

TALKING TO YOUR CHILD ABOUT THEIR AUTISM DIAGNOSIS

Chapter 1

ARE YOU READY FOR THE 'AUTISM TALK'?

When a child or adolescent is diagnosed with autism, it is often the result of many years of questions, visits to medical professionals, conflicting opinions and a great deal of concern and stress from parents just wanting to find out how to best help their child. The experience of going through the diagnostic process with your child can be emotional, exhausting and enlightening all at the same time, and can have a lasting impact on you as parents and the family as a whole.

Before you start the process of talking to your child about their autism, it is important to consider your own thoughts and feelings about their diagnosis.

Where are you in your journey?

Regardless of the time that has passed since your child received their diagnosis, talking about autism may still leave a lump in your throat or a tear in your eye. It is difficult for any parent to see their child struggle, and when you know your child has autism, and that they are likely to experience a range of difficulties, it can be hard to be positive, even if you are told that your child can have a bright future. In addition to these concerns, managing the day-to-day challenges resulting from your child's behavior, sensory needs and social difficulties can be physically and emotionally overwhelming.

Your feelings about your child's diagnosis can change from day to day, or even minute to minute, depending on what is happening in your life. Many of the parents I work with report they have had similar experiences while going through the diagnostic process with their child, and when reflecting on the weeks and years following the diagnosis. However, while it helps to know others can relate to your experiences, it is important to remember that your journey is specific to you, and no one can tell you what you should or shouldn't be feeling.

Reaction to your child's diagnosis

For some parents, receiving a diagnosis for their child may come as a relief. After struggling to find reasons for their child's behavior, finding out their child has autism provides answers to many questions and a level of understanding from others, often removing the burden of feeling like their child's behavior is their fault. For other parents, a child's diagnosis may result in a devastating realization that their child is not like other children and is going to need ongoing support. Of course, there are many parents who fall somewhere in the middle, feeling happy to finally know why their child is different, but also feeling worried for what the future will bring. Whatever your reaction, the journey toward understanding and acceptance is an ongoing one and receiving a diagnosis for your child is only the beginning.

Experiencing grief and loss

It may seem unusual to talk about grief in relation to your child's diagnosis, but it is a common element in the journey of all the parents of children with autism whom I work with. In fact, it is present in the journeys of most parents of children with special needs.

The sense of grief and loss that parents of children with autism often experience is associated with the loss of the child they thought they would have, and the loss of the future life they thought their child would lead. Most parents have dreams for their children, and when they find out their child has autism, whether at 2 years or 15 years, the dreams they had for their child may seem to be lost.

What is also different about the grief experienced by parents of children with autism is that it is described as non-finite or never-ending. While the traditional idea of grief is that it will lessen over time, the feeling of grief associated with your child's autism may be relatively nonexistent when you and your child are doing well, but resurface and catch you off guard at times when you are confronted with your child's challenges. Again, this experience is very personal, and some parents may be affected more than others, but it is helpful to be aware of how it impacts you and those around you, and to seek support to work through these feelings if you feel you need to. It is important to remember that although it can be hard, it is a normal part of bringing up a child with autism.

When thinking about how you may experience grief, it is also worth considering that differences are common in the way parents manage their grief. While some parents tend to manage their grief by talking to others about their feelings, dwelling on and thinking about their concerns, and trying to find the positives in situations, others are more likely to try to push past their feelings and take action to try to make things better for their child and family. These differences can lead to misunderstandings and resentment if one parent interprets the other's different reaction as uncaring or unhelpful.

This discord between parents can be fueled further when one parent feels that their partner is already under considerable emotional strain, and consequently does not want to burden them by talking about how they are feeling or seek support from them. When a person's main source of support is their partner, but they feel they can't talk to them about their concerns, they may be left feeling isolated and unsupported. Taking the time to communicate your thoughts and feelings clearly with your partner, and trying to understand their experience, can help you to manage your grief effectively and move forward in your journey. It can also be helpful to seek professional support individually or as a couple, if you feel your grief and experience of raising a child with autism is having a negative impact on your wellbeing or your relationship.

Knowing when you are ready to talk to your child about autism

After considering your feelings around your child's diagnosis and where you are in your journey, it is time to think about whether you are ready to talk to your child about their autism. Being aware of your feelings can assist you to choose a time when you feel that you can communicate about autism in a positive and unemotional way.

If you find that thinking about your child's autism leaves you feeling distressed or angry, or that you have not reached the part of your journey where you can accept their diagnosis, then you are probably not ready to talk, and that is alright. You don't want to have a discussion when you are angry or upset about something your child has done, or when you have received negative feedback or news and are experiencing a moment of grief. Your child will pick up on your emotion and think that there is something wrong and that having autism is a bad thing, and that's not the message we want to convey. As I said before, everyone's journey is different, and it is important to take the time you need to process your child's diagnosis before you talk to them about it.

Do you have someone who can support you to talk to your child?

If you don't feel you are ready to tell your child but you think they are ready to learn about their autism, or need to know about their diagnosis, then enlisting the help of a trusted professional, friend or family member to talk to your child can be a good solution. You might have a friend or a relative whom your child is close to, who is happy to talk to them about autism. Alternatively, you might have a therapist whom your child sees regularly, who can support them in exploring their diagnosis. The most important factor is that your child receives reliable and honest information about autism from a supportive adult.

If you do choose to have someone help with the process, it doesn't mean you can't be involved if you want to be. I have had many parents ask me to assist them to talk to their child about their diagnosis, and we have had the discussion all together, with the parent present. In this way, the parent can hear how autism is being presented to the child and see the child's reaction first hand, without having to find the words themselves.

Wherever you are in your journey with autism, taking the time to reflect on your own thoughts and feelings will help you make informed decisions about when and how to talk to your child about their diagnosis. Then, regardless of whether you tell them tomorrow, or in three years' time, you can be confident that the message your child receives about autism is a positive one.

Chapter 2

WHAT DO YOU KNOW ABOUT AUTISM?
FACT VS FICTION

Before you talk to your child about their diagnosis, it is important to have accurate information about what autism is and is not.

By definition, autism spectrum disorder is a neuro-developmental disorder characterized by impairments in social communication and interaction, and restricted and repetitive interests and behaviors. When we talk about impairments in social communication and interaction, we are talking about difficulties with social skills such as understanding emotions in ourselves and others, reading nonverbal cues including facial expressions and body language, having conversations, understanding another person's point of view, and making and maintaining friendships. With regard to restricted and repetitive interests and behaviors, these can include rigidity around routines, difficulties with transitions and change, repetitive play, intense interests in specific topics, and sensory sensitivities.

While we still have a lot to learn, the extensive research into autism spectrum disorder in recent years is helping us better understand what autism is and how it develops.

Fact: There is no single cause of autism

We know that there are differences in brain function in children with autism, but there does not appear to be one single cause. There are a lot of different factors that seem to contribute. There is definitely a genetic component, at least in families who have multiple children on the spectrum, and there are genetic syndromes that result in patterns of behaviors consistent with autism. In contrast, we also find that some families don't seem to have any family history of autism. I think in those children it could be a combination of traits that are present in other family members but not at a clinical level. For example, there might be an uncle who has some social difficulties and a cousin who has language difficulties and somebody else who has some other developmental issues, and for whatever reason it all comes together in one particular child at a clinical level and they meet the criteria for an autism diagnosis. Certainly there are also environmental factors being investigated that may contribute to the development of autism, but there have been no clear answers about what these are and how they work.

Fact: Autism is quite common in the community

The reported incidence of autism has changed quite a bit in recent years, with research suggesting around 1 in 88 children are born with autism. There are many theories regarding the apparent increase in children being diagnosed with autism. However, the most likely cause of increased numbers is the widening of diagnostic criteria to include more mildly affected individuals, and increased awareness and knowledge of the characteristics of autism amongst both parents and medical professionals. Regardless of the current research and statistics, in my experience it is rare for any preschool or school classroom not to have at least one child with autism in attendance, and it is just as rare to meet someone who doesn't have a connection with autism through family or friends.

Fact: Autism is a lifelong condition

There has been a recent shift in research focus from autism being considered a childhood disorder to a lifelong condition. Research has expanded from primarily looking at autism in early childhood to consideration of autism across the lifespan, with interest growing in learning how to support adults with autism to study, work and live independently, rather than just focusing on early diagnosis and intervention.

As autism is a neurological condition, it is characterized by differences in brain function that persist across the lifespan. The characteristics may reduce over time, and certainly with early intervention and additional support a lot of people learn to manage their difficulties more effectively in their day-to-day lives, but their autism is still there – it doesn't go away.

Fact: The presentation of autism in individuals is varied

The spectrum that we talk about is still very relevant with regards to the individual differences seen in people with autism.

While the pattern of impairments that make up the diagnostic criteria are consistent, the intensity and severity of those impairments varies with each child or adult. For example, one child with autism might prefer their own company and have an intense and all-encompassing interest in trains, whereas another child with autism may desperately want to have friends but not have the skills to play cooperatively with a peer and struggle to tolerate any changes in their daily routine. This is further illustrated by the severity in which individuals are impacted by their autistic characteristics. While some individuals appear to be more mildly affected and readily learn to manage their difficulties, others may struggle with all aspects of their day-to-day functioning and require constant adult care.

Fact: Children with autism can have quite varied cognitive abilities

When professionals talk about cognitive abilities, they are referring to a person's ability to think, understand, problem-solve and remember information. These abilities are collectively called intelligence or IQ. Cognitive abilities in children with autism can range from quite low to superior, with many kids falling in the average range. Children with autism often have splintered skills, meaning they might excel in some areas but struggle in others. While children with autism may at times develop strong skills in counting, reciting the alphabet and reading, it is the functional quality of these skills that is often impaired. The repetitive nature of these sequences of numbers and letters can be quickly mastered by rote. However, the ability to count with meaning and understanding, such as knowing that ten apples is more than five apples, or understanding the meaning of a word they just read, may be lacking, indicating a gap or a delay in development.

Fact: Girls with autism can present differently to boys

There are differing opinions about the number of girls with autism in the community compared to boys. However, increased awareness of the different ways girls with autism present has led to more girls receiving diagnoses in recent years. While some girls demonstrate a more classic presentation, others with average cognitive functioning and good language skills have been found to present with a more subtle profile.

One way in which girls can differ is in their social imitation skills. Better social imitation skills allow girls to appear more socially competent, when they are actually just copying the behavior of their peers. This can lead to later diagnosis in girls, because their social impairments do not become as evident until the gap widens between their skills and the skills of their peers, often toward the end of primary school.

Girls can also differ in the themes and intensity of their special interests. Girls are reported often to have interests that are age-appropriate and similar to peers, such as animals or books. However, the level of that interest can still be quite intense.

These differences, and several others that have been identified, are becoming more widely recognized and understood, resulting in better supports being created for girls with autism.

Fact: Many children with autism have sensory processing difficulties

Sensory processing difficulties can play a significant part in how children with autism experience the world around them and react to situations in their everyday life. Sensory processing involves the way in which the body and brain take in and interpret information from the senses. Contrary to popular belief, there are actually seven senses. There are the five senses most of us learned about at school – sight, hearing, touch, taste and smell – and there are also two other senses – proprioception (body awareness) and vestibular (balance and movement). The proprioceptive system uses information from the muscles and joints to tell the brain about where a certain body part is in relation to the rest of the body and how it is moving. The vestibular system uses information from the inner ear to tell the brain where our body is in space, and the speed and direction of our movement and the movement of our environment.

Many children with autism are either overstimulated or understimulated by sensory input coming from the seven sensory systems, resulting in them becoming easily overwhelmed and anxious, or alternatively under-responsive to the world around them. Understanding what types of sensory input your child seeks out or needs and what they find distressing or overwhelming can assist with managing challenging behavior, reducing anxiety and supporting learning.

Fact: Many children with autism experience high levels of anxiety

Given their difficulties understanding social interaction, the need for routine and familiarity, and the sensory sensitivities experienced by many people with autism, it is understandable that they would also experience anxiety in their daily lives. Further, the incidence of anxiety disorders in people with autism is reportedly as high as 40 percent, compared with around 15 percent in the general population.

There are several qualities characteristic of autism that appear to predispose individuals to experience anxiety. First, people with autism often have a narrow pattern of thinking that leads to a tendency to focus on detail rather than the bigger picture. This thinking pattern can make it more difficult to problem-solve and consider alternatives in challenging situations, and is also characteristic of neurotypical individuals with anxiety disorders.

Second, the sensory sensitivities experienced by many people with autism often elicit physical symptoms that mirror an anxiety response. When our bodies perceive a threat, our nervous system responds by releasing chemicals that cause physical symptoms including an increase in heart rate, nausea and rapid breathing. When a body is unable to process sensory information effectively, sensory overload can occur, triggering an extreme physical response and causing distress to the individual.

Lastly, the social and communication difficulties demonstrated by many people with autism can contribute to higher levels of anxiety in unfamiliar settings and social situations. Confusion or lack of understanding of social rules, difficulty expressing themselves and having their needs met, and problems managing transitions and unfamiliar environments can all lead to increased levels of anxiety.

Fiction: People with autism are not affectionate

While some children with autism do not like to be touched, others enjoy the opportunity for a hug and a cuddle. This will often be on their terms. They may not like to be approached, but when they feel like being close they will seek out their parent or carer to do this. Further, due to difficulties with social cues, some children with autism enjoy hugs so much they will indiscriminately hug any adult or child who is nearby or is nice to them.

It is also important to remember that people show affection in different ways, and people with autism are no different. While some may show affection with a kiss or a cuddle, for others, a short squeeze of a hand or a pat on the back may be their way of showing their love. As parents, we may need to adjust what our idea of affection is, but those small gestures can have a lot of meaning.

Fiction: People with autism do not have empathy

There are different views in the research community regarding empathy in individuals with autism. In my experience, the issue is not with the presence of empathy, which I think people with autism do have, but rather the ability to correctly interpret and respond to other people's emotions. Particularly in children with autism, their focus is on themselves and meeting their own needs, so they often do not automatically consider others and how they may be feeling or reacting to situations around them. Even when they do learn to recognize how someone else is feeling and care about their reaction, they may not know how to respond appropriately and therefore do not respond at all. For other children, their apparent lack of empathy may be more to do with difficulties with Theory of Mind. Theory of Mind is the ability to see things from another person's perspective and understand that others have separate thoughts and feelings from our own. When people with autism have poor Theory of Mind, they have difficulty recognizing that others think differently to themselves and therefore their apparent lack of empathy could be more about having trouble understanding others' perspectives than not caring about others. For example, they may see someone fall over and think it looks funny so they laugh, assuming that the person who has fallen over would think it is funny too. Their poor Theory of Mind means they don't understand that the other person could be experiencing the situation differently and doesn't think it is funny at all.

In contrast to those individuals who have difficulty showing empathy, some children with autism experience empathy at an extreme level, becoming very distressed when they see or hear others upset or in pain. This extreme emotional response can then sometimes be all-consuming, making the child unable to demonstrate their empathy toward someone else due to their own distress.

Fiction: People with autism do not want to have friends

There still appears to be a common belief by some in the community that children with autism are not interested in interacting with others and are happier playing on their own.

While this may be true for some, many children with autism do want to have friends, but may not have the skills they need to be successful in forming peer relationships. For example, a child wanting to join in a game of basketball in the playground may run in and take the ball his peers are playing with to get their attention, instead of walking over and asking if they can play. When a child with autism is unsuccessful in their efforts to make friends, or is rejected by peers, they can become socially isolated, not by choice but by their circumstance.

Fiction: People are not born with autism – it's just bad parenting

Bad parenting does not cause autism. The challenging behaviors exhibited by autistic children are part of their condition and are not due to parenting style. The idea that parents need to say 'no' more or 'punish' their children to 'fix' their autism is misguided and unhelpful, as it places undue pressure and blame on parents for their child's behavior.

Children need to be taught how to behave appropriately. It is okay to have expectations for a child's behavior and for their behavior to have consequences, but these need to be appropriate and reasonable. While there are strategies that we know will assist with behavior management, such as being firm, calm and consistent, we also know that some 'typical' ways of disciplining children do not work with children with autism. Strategies need to be tailored to an individual child's cognitive and communication skills. For example, there is no point in sending a child to 'time out' for bad behavior, when they have no understanding of what they have done wrong.

Fiction: Children with autism are just being naughty

All behavior is communication, and difficult behavior by a child with an autism diagnosis is their way of expressing themselves (e.g. their difficult behavior may exist to highlight their distress, discomfort, annoyance, excitement).

While a child may appear to be doing something just to annoy others or be 'naughty,' most children with autism are acting on their own agenda – they do things to meet their own needs. It's not about others; it's about them getting what they want or need. That being said, it is important that children with autism learn the appropriate way to manage their emotions and express themselves. But they need to be taught, and it takes time – they don't just pick it up on their own.

Fiction: Autism can be cured

There is no cure for autism, and it would be argued by many people with autism and their families that autism does not need to be cured. Instead, it needs to be understood and accepted.

There are therapies that are effective at reducing some children's challenging behaviors and autistic characteristics, as well as ways to teach and develop skills to function effectively in the world, but autism is a neurodevelopmental disorder that indicates a difference in neurological function. Those differences in brain structure and function are permanent and will not disappear over time.

While we are aware of many therapies that do assist people with autism to overcome or manage their difficulties, there are also a lot of alternative therapies that are not based on appropriate evidence and that can be harmful. It is important to educate yourself, to be aware of the pros and cons of any intervention or treatment, and not to be drawn in by unrealistic claims. If it sounds too good to be true, you need to consider that it might actually not be true.

Chapter 3

WHY TELL YOUR CHILD THEY HAVE AUTISM?

Is it important to tell a child they have autism? Do they need to know? Will they figure it out for themselves? What does the future look like if they don't know?

These are questions that parents of children with autism may ask themselves many times from the time their child receives their diagnosis, and the answer is not a straightforward one. Depending on who you talk to, there are different opinions on whether it is necessary to tell your child about their autism or not.

When I talk to parents about this question, some say to me that they don't feel it is necessary for their child to know, because their child is doing well, and they are concerned that telling them they have autism might jeopardize their progress. Other parents feel it is a natural thing to talk to their child about their autism and how it influences their life in both positive and negative ways.

I believe that telling your child about their autism is about providing a missing piece of a puzzle. Without that piece, the puzzle is incomplete. For a child with autism, giving them information about their diagnosis gives them the opportunity to have a deeper understanding of who they are.

When thinking about whether to tell your child about their diagnosis, the following factors will be important to consider.

Autism is part of who they are

I think it is important for children who do receive a diagnosis to know and understand that autism is a part of who they are as a person. They need to know that there is something different about the way their brain works, that it means that they sometimes see and interpret things differently, and that it is not something they need to change about themselves, because it is the way they are made.

This becomes even more important for children to know as they grow older and are developing a sense of identity. As children grow and develop, they gather information about themselves and the people around them to develop a sense of who they are and where they fit. They look for similarities between themselves and others, comparing their abilities and achievements with their peers and taking cues from the important adults in their lives to assess their self-worth. When children have difficulty relating to others, find themselves getting into trouble for their behavior but don't really understand why, or feel their abilities don't compare with their peers, their self-esteem and self-worth can suffer.

Giving children with autism information that explains why they may have these challenges, and helping them to be aware of autistic adults whom they can look up to, can assist them to develop a more positive view of themselves and their abilities.

Knowing can reduce the fear that something is wrong with them

A lot of children with autism reach a point when they know that they are different. They may have an idea that they have a bit of trouble with some things, and that they're a little bit different to the other kids in their class. Some children – particularly children in mainstream settings – may start to worry that there is something wrong with them and question why they are different. When questions are ignored or are not honestly answered, or the child is too afraid to ask, the child will often seek information themselves, which may lead them to the wrong conclusions.

This can be further complicated by peers noticing differences and making comments about a child's abilities or behaviors. Children report being told that there is 'something wrong with their brain,' that they are 'dumb' or 'stupid,' and even that 'they are aliens.' These types of comments can highlight the differences the child is already aware of, prompt new concerns or serve to confirm the child's own fears that there is something wrong with them.

Receiving an explanation of why they are different can be a big relief for some children. It can help them really understand their behavior and thinking, and why they may struggle with some things, and reassure them that there is not something terribly wrong with them. Further, their differences do not have to be seen as negatives. While their autism may be the reason why their thinking sometimes gets stuck or they sometimes have trouble having a conversation with someone, it is also the reason they have an amazing memory for things they are interested in or notice some things more than other people. These qualities or behaviors, which can play a huge part in the child's day-to-day life, become clearer and make sense to them once they understand their diagnosis. This can help the child in learning to accept all parts of themselves – the good parts and the not-so-good parts – and be more confident and happy about their place in the world.

A parent telling their child is better than someone else telling them

Many parents find themselves feeling pushed to tell their child about their diagnosis due to another child finding out, and the parents not wanting their child to hear about it somewhere else first. I have had many conversations with concerned parents over the years – parents who are stressed because another parent or sometimes a teacher has revealed a child's diagnosis to someone else; meanwhile the child doesn't know about their autism because their parent was waiting for the 'right time.' When this occurs, the conversation with the child can end up being reactive and rushed, rather than the parent having time to really consider what information they want to share and how to share it.

This was the situation I found myself in before my youngest son, Aaron, who has autism, started school. Aaron had visited his school many times with his older brother, Sean, and the other kids in Sean's grade had recognized there was something different about him. As there was another child in Sean's grade with autism, some of his classmates joined the dots and were talking about Aaron having autism too. When Sean came home and asked me whether Aaron had autism, I knew I needed to say something, as I didn't want other children to know about Aaron's diagnosis if he didn't know himself. This marked the start of Aaron's journey in understanding his diagnosis.

The difficulty with someone else mentioning autism first is that it may occur in a negative way, or the information that is given may be slightly inaccurate or just completely wrong. This is likely to cause confusion and distress, and will make it more difficult to discuss autism in a positive way later on.

Preparing to tell a child about their diagnosis before it is shared with others provides parents with an opportunity to present information in a clear, positive and age-appropriate way, and makes it less likely that misunderstanding or distress will occur.

Knowing increases participation in therapy and acceptance of strategies to help them

When a child understands why they need assistance with skills such as making friends or having conversations, they are often more willing to participate in therapy. With the knowledge that they have autism, a child is more likely to see that going and learning about how to make friends, or learning about how to write better, or how to cope with some of their sensory sensitivities, is actually going to help them.

Attending therapy without really knowing why can lead to the child resenting the sessions because attending means missing out on other activities. Some children may feel that they don't need to attend and don't need any help, resulting in them being uncooperative or resistant to suggestions being made to help them. Rather than being resistant to being involved in therapy, children who are aware of their autism and the difficulties they have are often better able to work with their therapist to find the best way to help them achieve their potential, and work through problems that are most relevant to them.

Being knowledgeable about their diagnosis also empowers children as they get older to have a say in what support they need and the most effective way for them to receive it. I find that with most children with autism, there are always things we can be working on and learning about in sessions, but that is not always what a child or their family needs. Sometimes it is about the child having a break from therapy to use and consolidate their skills in the real world, or moving on to another therapist who can support them with their changing needs as they get older; and often it is the child with autism who can let us know when the time is right to make a change.

This idea is well illustrated by an email I recently received from a parent of one of my clients, a 12-year-old boy with Asperger syndrome, called Tom. We had been working together for more than two years, developing strategies to help him manage his anxiety at school and in the community, and building up his skills in social problem-solving. He had a lot of insight into his diagnosis, and had made some fantastic gains, successfully applying the strategies he had learned in sessions when out in the real world. Tom was about to move on to secondary school, and had been considering his need for therapy in the coming year. He told his mother that he felt he had gone as far as he could with me, and thought a male psychologist would be more helpful for him moving into secondary school. While I was sad to see him move on, I was thrilled that he had been able to consider his own future needs and felt confident to discuss making a change. If he wasn't aware of his diagnosis and why he was seeing a psychologist, it is unlikely he would have had the insight to make a change when it was needed.

It can give them a place where they belong

For a child who may feel like they never really fit in, knowing that they have autism, and that there are other children like them, can make a big difference to their self-confidence and self-esteem. Obviously not all children with autism are going to get along with each other, just like not all neurotypical children get along, but finding someone with similar interests and perspectives, and knowing that others have similar challenges, can help children feel that they are not alone.

With the knowledge that they have autism, children and adolescents can seek out peers to connect with in social groups and recreational activities, creating networks of like-minded individuals who can encourage and support them. Opportunities to meet and be mentored by autistic adults can also assist children to look toward possibilities for the future. Many autism support organizations offer social groups or support groups for children and adults with autism, which allow individuals to socialize and develop connections with others in safe and supportive environments. In Melbourne, Australia, where I live and work, there are a number of organizations making a difference in bringing people with autism together in both social and mentoring programs. The 'I Can Network,' founded by Chris Varney in 2013, is one of these organizations. Following the interest created by his TedX talk in Melbourne, 'Autism – How My Unstoppable Mother Proved the Experts Wrong,' Chris and several friends and colleagues who also have autism started an organization that aims to empower individuals with autism by mentoring them to live with an 'I can' attitude and embrace their autism. Chris and his team regularly speak at schools, universities, community and corporate events and conferences, spreading their message about what people with autism can do, and running camps, events and individual mentoring sessions for people with autism, to encourage them to reach their potential. Organizations like these are helping children with autism grow up knowing there are other people like them in the world, and showing them what they can achieve when they put their mind to it.

While there is no guarantee that a child will accept their diagnosis immediately, given time, support and information, it is likely that they will develop an understanding of what having autism means for them. With that understanding can come a stronger sense of self and a clearer picture of where they fit in the world, helping them feel confident to strive to reach their potential.

Chapter 4

WHEN IS THE RIGHT TIME TO TALK TO YOUR CHILD ABOUT THEIR DIAGNOSIS?

As a psychologist, one of the most common questions I am asked by parents when discussing talking about a diagnosis is: "When should I tell them?" There are different opinions regarding when a child should be told, but there is no 'perfect time.' For me, the 'right time' depends on the child and the family and what works best for them.

In deciding when to talk to your child about their diagnosis, there are a few things that can be helpful to consider.

Earlier is better

Children don't need to be told by a specific age, but it is generally thought that earlier is better. Obviously, there are big differences in the ages that individuals are diagnosed with autism spectrum disorder – some as young as 18 months and others not until they reach adolescence or adulthood – so the time that an individual can be told varies considerably. I think that the notion of telling a child or adolescent early in their journey allows for greater growth and understanding of what autism means for them.

It is an ongoing process or journey

When you introduce your child to their autism, you are not going to sit down and have a five-minute conversation with your child and then not have to talk about it again. The conversation, however you choose to start it, will be an ongoing process that evolves over time, as your child's understanding of autism develops.

My own journey discussing autism with my son started when he was 5 years old and has taken many twists and turns over the years. Questions such as "Where is my autism kept?" and "Does my teacher know I have autism?" were answered as best I could, when they were asked, with positivity and factual information. Now 13 years old, he has a much better understanding of his autism, but I know there are more questions and a deeper understanding still to come.

As children get older, their questions are likely to be more complex, and it is important that they have people they can go to in order to receive reliable and factual information. Linking a child or adolescent with a mentor who has autism, to provide information that is real and relevant, can be very useful and empowering to the child. Seeking support from professionals with understanding and experience of autism, and educating yourself about autism and the experiences of autistic children and adolescents, can also assist you to be able to answer questions when they come up or help find the answer if you don't have it yourself.

Choose the time that is right for you, your child and your family

There are several different approaches to choosing when to tell your child about their diagnosis. Some parents discuss autism immediately, from the time of diagnosis; others may wait until their child is a certain age or developmental level, or starts to ask questions about differences between themselves and their peers. As I have said earlier, the right time depends on the individual, so I will discuss each of these approaches to help you find one that works best for you and your family.

TAKING YOUR CUE FROM YOUR CHILD

Some professionals and parents say that talking to your child about their diagnosis when they are aware of difference in themselves and other children is a really good time.

When they are asking questions like "Why is it hard to make friends?" or "Why do I have to go to appointments all the time?" they have obviously become aware that they are not doing things the same as some other children. How great that awareness is may differ, but if they have that understanding and they're curious about that, it is a really good opportunity to bring up the subject of autism and talk to them about it. If they are asking questions, it is hoped they are ready for whatever answers you have for them.

Alternatively, they might not be directly asking questions but they might be noticing and commenting on differences between themselves and others – for example, that they are taller than some other kids at their kindergarten or some of the kids at school wear glasses and others don't. Obviously, unlike autism, those differences can be seen, but that awareness of physical differences gives you an opportunity to start to bring up why they themselves might be a bit different to other kids.

We will discuss how to talk to your child in the next chapter, but it is important to note that the conversation about autism does not have to start by using the word 'autism' if you are not comfortable with that. There are many other ways to describe differences and abilities that can be used to introduce what autism is without giving it a name. The name can come later.

TALKING ABOUT AUTISM FROM DAY ONE

Another option is to talk about autism from day one, that is, from the time of diagnosis. The idea is to make the word 'autism' just a part of everyday conversation and use it to describe things that the child is doing, to explain why they may or may not be able to do something or why they need to see professionals such as psychologists and speech pathologists.

Stephen Shore, a professor of special education at Adelphi University, and an author and autism advocate, described in an interview with Dr. Neal Goodman from Boston Children's Hospital that his parents just talked about his autism in a matter-of-fact way for as long as he could remember.

"It was very matter of fact," he explained. "My parents used my diagnosis to explain things to me, like 'That's why you're going to the Putnam School' or 'That's why you're going to the doctor today.'" When asked about his initial reaction when his parents told him about his diagnosis, he said, "I saw autism as no big deal. It was just matter-of-fact."

Making the word 'autism' part of your everyday vocabulary can help a child accept that autism is just a part of their life and is nothing to be scared or ashamed of. It can also assist other family members to understand the child's strengths and challenges in relation to their autism in a more normalized way.

Waiting until your child has the capacity to understand the diagnosis

For some parents, waiting for a time when their child is likely to understand what having autism means, feels like the best option. This will vary greatly between individuals, and will depend on the child or adolescent's cognitive and language abilities, as well as how engaged and aware they are of their environment.

It is important also to consider what it is you want your child to understand. If you only want them to have an understanding that the word 'autism' applies to them in some way, then this may happen early in a child's development. However, if you want your child to understand more specific information about autism, such as its neurobiological basis and the pattern of behaviors that characterize it, then it is likely that waiting until your child is older will be necessary, and the information will need to be tailored to the child's developmental level.

While in some cases, individuals may never develop the ability to understand their diagnosis fully, I think it is important that they are still given the opportunity to have awareness of their autism in whatever way they are able.

Involving your child in the diagnostic process

For school-aged children and adolescents, the diagnostic process can be experienced in vastly different ways. For some, it is an opportunity to do special activities with a professional who is totally engaged and interested in them. For others, it can be a source of stress and confusion, as the child is being 'tested' for a reason they may not fully understand.

Even when a child has not been told they are being assessed, they are often able to pick up on the fact that they are visiting multiple doctors and professionals and have a sense that there is something going on. A great example of this is an 8-year-old girl who was coming to me for some help with social skills and anxiety. After a few sessions, her parents decided that they would like to do some more formal assessment to investigate a possible autism diagnosis. As she was used to our sessions running in a particular way, I explained that we had some different things to do one session, and we completed a play-based autism assessment. Even though no one had mentioned assessment to her, on the way home in the car she told her mother that she had done a test with me that day.

If your child is old enough to be aware of the process, talking to them about the fact that they are seeing some professionals to help figure out how they can be best supported at school and at home, or to assist them with some of the difficulties they may be experiencing, can be a great way to broach the topic of assessment. Then, if your child does receive an autism diagnosis, you can further that discussion by explaining what kind of information was gathered during the assessment and what that means for them.

Whenever you decide to talk to your child about their diagnosis, it is important that you have accurate information and feel confident to give your child a positive message about their autism. The following chapters will give you the tools you need to talk to your child about their diagnosis in a positive and empowering way.

Chapter 5

HOW DO YOU TELL YOUR CHILD ABOUT THEIR AUTISM?

As a parent, you know your child better than anyone else, and that knowledge can assist you to talk to your child about their autism in a way that suits their needs. When you are going to talk to your child about their diagnosis, it is good to think about how you can best communicate with them in order to promote understanding. Below are some things to consider regarding how to communicate your message about autism effectively.

Tailor the information to your child's developmental level

It is important that you target the information that you are giving your child to their developmental level. You need to think about their use and understanding of language, and whether their strengths are in verbal or nonverbal communication. If you give your child a complicated description of autism when they are not ready for it, they are not likely to understand it and might become confused. However, if you are too simple in your description, a child who has the capacity to understand more complex concepts may feel they are being talked down to and refuse to listen or be part of the conversation. Try to find a balance between what you want them to know about autism and how much they can process and understand; and once you get started, don't be afraid to change direction if you feel that your child needs more or less information or a different approach.

For younger children, or children who are developmentally delayed, using pictures, stories and familiar characters from television or movies can be a great way of helping them to understand and relate to what you are telling them. There are some wonderful picture books and video clips available that present autism in different ways, and can be used to introduce the topic of autism to your child. For example, the recent addition of 'Julia' to the Sesame Street family provides a wonderful way to talk about autism, and perhaps discuss how your child may be similar or different to her. Books like *Me and My Brain: Ellie's Story*, by Antoniette Preston and Kerryn Lisa, also introduce autism in a child-friendly way.

For older children, books, videos and diagrams can be used to engage them and introduce information about autism. You can then discuss autism in more detail and answer any questions they might have about what they have seen or heard. Online videos of children with autism talking about their experiences can also be a great way of introducing information in a relatable way, provided you have seen the video first and are confident that the content is appropriate. One video that comes to mind is a BBC documentary called *My Autism and Me*. The documentary is hosted by 13-year-old Rosie King, a young girl with Asperger syndrome, and she discusses her experiences and the experiences of a number of other autistic children with different presentations and abilities. Rosie also presented a talk at TEDMED 2014 when she was 16 years old, which is readily available online (see Chapter 17, videos for family and friends) and gives further insight into her thoughts on what it means to have autism.

If your child prefers to read, there is also a range of books targeting older children that can help them navigate their thoughts and feelings about having autism. A list of books suitable for different ages and stages of development is included in Chapter 17.

Be honest

When you talk to your child about autism, be honest with them. You want your child to trust what you are telling them and feel confident in the information you give them, and being honest is the best way to do that.

While you may need to keep things simple, you should still be clear about the facts. It is important to be truthful in talking about both the good and the not-so-good aspects of having autism. Your child needs to know that there may be challenges, but there will also be great things that they can do that their autism may even help them with. What you don't want to do is give your child incorrect or misleading information that creates a problem for them or for yourself in the future. For example, it might seem like a novel idea to tell your child their autism is a superpower when they are 5 years old, but it is likely that it will not be well received when they are 10 and trying to explain autism to their peers. Sticking to the facts will help your child to have the best possible understanding of autism at whatever stage they are in their development.

An example of this is a story a parent told me about their 8-year-old son with autism. He was told about his diagnosis by his parents after a peer at school told him he had 'something wrong with his brain' and his parents didn't want him to feel bad about being different. They explained to him that there was nothing wrong with his brain; it was just different, and there were a lot of things that his brain could do well. Now, whenever anyone says anything negative about him or his diagnosis, he tells them confidently that there is nothing wrong with him and that his autism makes his brain smart.

Be positive

Living with autism is not easy. In fact, I know from both my personal and professional experience that living with autism can be a real struggle, not just for the child with autism but also for their family. There are aspects of autism that I think many parents would gladly take away if they could – the communication difficulties, the sensory sensitivities, the anxiety, the loneliness. However, there are also aspects of autism that most would not want to change for the world. These qualities are the things that we want children with autism to embrace and be proud of.

So, when you are talking to your child about their autism – a condition that they are born with and will have for their whole life – it is important to focus on the positives. Having autism doesn't mean that your child can't achieve their potential. Some children are going to need more help than others, but they can all achieve, and we want them to be positive about that. You can focus on the positives by not only talking about what your child is good at, but also how they can manage their challenges effectively.

For example, your child might have a fantastic memory, have great sporting skills and know a lot about dinosaurs, but have difficulty making friends and managing noisy environments. With some help and guidance they can learn to make friends; it is just that it doesn't come as naturally for them as it does for other children. They can also learn to cope better in noisy situations but they might need earplugs or to be gradually exposed to that environment until they can tolerate it.

Putting a positive focus on your child's autism doesn't mean you don't acknowledge their struggles, but instead it means you can help your child to see all the possibilities that their future holds.

Be matter of fact

Finally, when you are talking to your child about their autism, think about the message you are going to convey with your tone of voice and the emotion that is behind it. Using a matter-of-fact, neutral tone in your voice when you talk about autism will communicate to your child that the information you are sharing is not something they should be worried or concerned about. If you take the emotion out of your voice and talk in a way that is conversational, you are normalizing the situation and the information that is being provided to them. I think that when children receive information in this way, it is more likely that they will take what you have said on board and process it in a neutral way. Then it is hoped that they will be able to acknowledge the facts that you have given them and take the time they need to figure out what it means for them.

Being clear about the best way to communicate with your child about their diagnosis will make the process much easier and give your child the best possible chance of understanding how autism relates to them.

Chapter 6

WHAT DO YOU TELL YOUR CHILD ABOUT THEIR AUTISM?

Once you have decided that you want to tell your child about their autism, there are certain things that I think are important for your child to know – things that are fundamental to their understanding of autism and what it means for them. You might tell them during your first conversation about autism, or later down the track when your child is developing a better understanding of what autism is. Regardless of when you choose to tell them, you should share this information in whatever way you feel they will best understand.

Your child is a child first

Your child is still the person they have always been. They are not suddenly different once they receive their diagnosis, and it is important for them to know that. What we want a child to understand and accept is that autism is a part of who they are but it doesn't necessarily define them. Their diagnosis helps us better understand the way they think and some of their needs, but they are still their own person and can choose how they want to see themselves.

A great way to explain this is to think about autism as an ingredient that helps makes the child who they are. This is a concept that was first introduced to me through the Facebook page 'I Am Cadence' by 8-year-old Cadence, a young girl with autism. Cadence drew a picture that was posted on her page, illustrating that autism should be considered an ingredient not a label, and listing her ingredients. In my own private practice, I have found that this is a wonderful way of helping children understand where autism fits into their image of themselves. I encourage them to draw a picture of themselves in the center of a page, and then list all the qualities or 'ingredients' that make them who they are around their picture, including autism as one of those qualities.

When children can see that autism is just one part of them, it can help them put their diagnosis in perspective and view it in a more positive light. It can also help them see that there are more similarities than differences between themselves and their peers.

Your child is not alone

It is important for any child to feel a sense of belonging, and children with autism are no exception. Knowing you are different can be hard, but knowing that there are others who share your differences and understand your challenges can make it a lot easier to manage.

It is very common nowadays to walk into a classroom and find at least one child with autism among the students. Letting your child know that many other children have autism, including children at their kindergarten or school, can help them feel that their differences are not rare or unusual.

One way to introduce this idea is to ask your child if they know anyone who is similar to them at school or kindergarten. Often, when given this question, they will mention children who do indeed have a diagnosis or are likely to be on the spectrum. One of the families I work with recounted a story recently of having this conversation with their 7-year-old daughter, Sophie, during a car trip. We had spoken to Sophie about her autism diagnosis during an individual session several weeks earlier, and she had asked about it on several occasions since. On this particular day, Sophie asked her mother about other people who have autism. Her mother mentioned that there were some kids at school who had autism whom she knew, and told her their names, and they talked about how Sophie was similar to them in some ways and different in others. One thing that Sophie particularly related to with regard to her autism is her emotional sensitivity, and she mentioned during the conversation that her younger sister also has this quality. This was particularly insightful, as her sister also has an autism diagnosis but has not yet been told about this. Overall, this discussion helped Sophie understand that she was not alone in having autism amongst her peers, which gave her a real sense of belonging.

When talking to your child about people they know with autism, remember to make sure that anyone with autism whom you mention already knows about their diagnosis. You don't want to place another family in a situation where their child is told about autism by someone else, or have them react in a negative way if your child mentions autism to them.

For older children, it can be useful to mention peers or adults in the community or even celebrities who have autism, to highlight a sense of commonality and the possibility for a successful future. Hearing stories from individuals with autism themselves can also be encouraging and reassuring. For example, talking about actors like Dan Aykroyd and Daryl Hannah, who have spoken publicly about receiving an autism diagnosis and the challenges they have faced, can help young people see that autism does not have to limit their potential. Books such as *Different Like Me: My Book of Autism Heroes* by Jennifer Elder, which highlights well-known figures in history who are thought to have had autism, and personal accounts of growing up with autism such as *Freaks, Geeks and Asperger Syndrome* by Luke Jackson and *Pretending to Be Normal* by Liane Holliday Willey, can also help to acknowledge the challenges people with autism face as well as normalizing their experiences.

Your child was born with autism

Another important point for children to understand is that they were born with autism. We want them to know they have always had autism; they didn't catch it from someone or get it because they have done something wrong – it is just the way they are made.

One way to explain this is to talk about your child's brain working differently. This can be particularly helpful when explaining autism to young children or children with developmental delays, but it can be a useful explanation for older children too.

I find that talking about their brain and how it works differently due to their autism is a simple way of helping kids understand what autism actually means to them, especially because autism is an invisible condition. Children with autism don't look different to their siblings or the kids at school, but the differences in their brain cause them to see and process things differently, and their perception of the world can be different too.

When we are talking about this brain difference, we also want our children to know that different does not mean wrong. Having a brain that works differently doesn't mean your child can't do what everyone else does; it just means they may go about it in a different way. Though there may be challenges to thinking about things in a different way than your peers, there may also be definite advantages.

To assist with your explanation of brains working differently, it can be useful to use diagrams and visuals, which can be effective tools to use with both younger and older children (see Chapter 16 for downloadable worksheets). For younger children, you can compare differences in several ways. To illustrate differences in the way brains work, machine analogies are often really well received and understood. For example, you might compare a steam engine and a diesel engine. They both have moving parts, run on rails and require fuel to run, but their internal workings are different and so are their jobs. Steam engines are good at moving carriages; diesel engines are good at moving cargo. A steam engine can do the job of a diesel, but it will use a lot more fuel and have to work a lot harder. Similarly, while an autistic brain can do everything a neurotypical brain can do, sometimes it will take more work and energy.

Another analogy that could be used to illustrate differences in how the brain processes information is the idea of different travel routes to get from one place to another. A neurotypical brain would be illustrated by a more direct route from A to B, perhaps made by a car, whereas an autistic brain might be illustrated by a more indirect route that takes more twists and turns, such as a bus route. Both routes get from A to B successfully, but one takes more time and energy. Similarly, there may be times where an autistic brain takes more time and energy to achieve the same outcome as a neurotypical brain.

In each of these analogies, it is important to highlight that when the autistic brain is doing a task it is built for, it does it really well. It is only when it has to do something that is outside its range of usual skills that it takes more energy or support.

To further illustrate the idea that people with autism often have different perceptions of situations, you can use optical illusions. What a person sees in an optical illusion is not wrong, but it can be different to what another person sees. There are many pictures readily available in books and online that feature ambiguous-looking images that can be interpreted as different things depending on how you look at them (e.g. duck/rabbit, witch/lady, faces/vase). This is what we want children with autism to understand – different is not wrong; it's just different.

For older children, using the common analogy of computer operating systems can be a great way of representing differences in the workings of the brain. For example, while both laptops and tablets have many of the same functions and can accommodate many of the same games, each has a different operating system that allows it to process information and complete tasks. One system is not necessarily better than the other; they are just different.

Your child can learn how to manage challenges

Finally, while we acknowledge that having autism comes with challenges, we really want children with autism to understand that they can learn strategies to help manage the things they have trouble with. We don't want a child to think that having autism means they can't do things. What we want is for them to understand that there are things that other children might naturally learn to do that they have difficulty with, and they might need help to figure out how to do those things correctly or more appropriately.

For example, your child might need help making friends, or need to practice their handwriting, or they might need to use a special cushion to keep them sitting still in their seat at school, and that's all okay. It is important for them to understand that there are no limitations placed on them; they can find ways of accommodating difficulties that they have, and use their strengths to manage their challenges.

One way you can illustrate this idea to your child is to help them make a list of their strengths and challenges. Starting with a piece of paper divided into two columns, help your child list their strengths in the first column. If they have difficulty thinking of anything, or have a very short list, make some suggestions of your own. Once you have a list of strengths, help your child think of some things they find challenging, and list them in the second column.

With your child's list of strengths and challenges, you have an opportunity to talk to your child about how they can use some of their strengths to help them with the things they find challenging. For example, your child may list their computer skills as a strength, and handwriting as a challenge, so you could talk to them about using their computer skills to manage their handwriting difficulties by typing some of their school work. For the challenges they can't use strengths to overcome, you can discuss other ways of managing these difficulties, including learning new skills or finding ways to make accommodations.

If you think this activity could be difficult for your child, or that they will need an example of what to do before they try it, you can start by creating a list of your own strengths and challenges, or those of a family member or friend, and having your child help you through each step. Once they understand the process, you can then get your child involved in making a list for themselves.

Now that you know what kind of information your child needs to understand autism, and have some ideas about how the information can be presented, you can start to plan how and when you will introduce your child to their diagnosis. In the upcoming chapters, I will share the stories of real families who have discussed their child's autism diagnosis at different times and in different ways, and give you an idea of what the 'Autism Talk' with your child might look like.

Chapter 7

A PERSONAL JOURNEY

Before I share the stories of some of the wonderful families I have worked with over the last ten years, I would like to share the story of how I came to tell my own son, Aaron, about his autism. I hope it will give you a picture of how your child's understanding of their autism will develop over time, and illustrate the idea that you will not have just one conversation about autism with your child. It is a process that you will go through together.

As I mentioned in Chapter 3, my decision to tell Aaron was the result of his older brother and other children at his school noticing Aaron's differences. They recognized similarities between Aaron and a girl already at the school who had an autism diagnosis, and used the word 'autism' to describe Aaron. This led to my older son asking me if Aaron had autism and started me on my journey of finding a way to explain Aaron's diagnosis to him in a simple and positive way.

So, when Aaron was 5 years old and about to start school, the opportunity arose to introduce the idea of autism while we were going for a drive in the car. Looking back, I'm not sure how the subject came up, but we started talking about autism and I said to Aaron that he had autism too. His reaction was simple: "I don't have autism, do I Mum?" I thought about how I might explain it better and said "You know how sometimes you have a little bit of trouble with your talking. That's because of your autism." Aaron replied, "But I don't have trouble with my talking, do I Mom?"

At that point I realized that he wasn't ready for a full explanation. It was enough that he had heard the word 'autism' associated with his talking, and it had come from me. I restated that autism was a way to describe that he sometimes had some difficulty with his talking, and left it at that. Over the course of the next few months, Aaron developed an understanding that the word 'autism' described a part of him, but what that meant for him was something that he hadn't quite worked out.

A year or so later, after having a meltdown, Aaron said to me, "I hate that I have autism. It makes me get upset," and went on to tell me he just didn't want to have it and he wanted it to go away. This was the first time he had associated anything negative with his autism. It also signified another step in his development, as he could see that his emotional reactions to things were different to those of other children. We talked about how he could learn to manage his emotions better and we just needed to practice. I also reassured him that having autism wasn't a bad thing and he just needed help with things sometimes. Then he went back to his toys and didn't want to talk any more.

I think Aaron was in Grade 3, about 8 years old, when he first tried to use his autism as an excuse. After being asked why he had not put his dishes in the sink like I had asked him to do, he said, "But I'm just a kid with autism." This took me by surprise, as he had not talked about autism in that way before, but I was quick to make it clear that having autism didn't mean he could get away with not doing things. "Yes, you have autism," I said, "but that doesn't mean that you can't do things that everyone else can do." He considered this and I could see his mind ticking over. Then he asked, "But does my teacher know that I have autism?" I think he had realized he couldn't use autism as an excuse at home, but thought maybe he could try it at school. He was possibly a little disappointed when I told him that his teacher knew about his diagnosis, and that he couldn't use autism as an excuse at school either, but I believe this discussion was another defining part of Aaron's journey. He was figuring out what his autism meant to him, and perhaps what it meant to others as well.

As Aaron was getting older, his understanding of autism continued to develop, and with it came more questions. "Where is my autism kept?" was probably the most interesting of all the questions he asked me. This prompted a conversation about the fact that his brain worked a bit differently to other children because of his autism, and that meant that he saw and processed things a bit differently. It was also an opportunity to talk about some other differences that were associated with his autism – that he would sometimes get upset about things that might not upset someone else; that he really loved Thomas the Tank Engine and knew everything about it – and help him understand and reinforce the fact that autism was just a part of who he is.

It was also around this time, when Aaron was in Grade 4, that the topic of different types of autism came up. I was watching the Louis Theroux documentary *Extreme Love – Autism* (Dir. Jamie Pickup, BBC Productions 2012), and Aaron walked in to see a teenage boy having an aggressive meltdown on the television. Seeing the boy in such distress, Aaron asked me what was wrong with the boy. I told him that the boy had autism, just like him, but that there were different types of autism that could affect kids in different ways. The easiest way for me to explain it to Aaron was to say that some children with autism have a lot of difficulty learning and may not be able to talk, like the boy on the television, but that Aaron's autism didn't affect his learning and he was able to manage his emotions and behavior better. Aaron seemed to accept this quite readily, and he did not ask me anything more about it.

Heading toward the end of primary school, Aaron was much more open in talking about his autism, particularly around the fact that I worked with a lot of children like him in early childhood and school settings. This further change in Aaron's acceptance of his diagnosis is beautifully illustrated in a story a friend of mine recounted. She had taken both my boys and her sons, who are similar ages, out to mini golf. My eldest son was telling his friends on the way home that I used to work nearby, and then I started studying to help Aaron. Aaron then spoke up in a matter-of-fact way and said, "Because I was born with autism." Interestingly, my friend's youngest son, who had been with Aaron since preschool and was now with him in Grade 5, said to his mom afterwards, "I didn't know Aaron had autism." He'd been with Aaron right through school, and Aaron knew about his diagnosis, but it was not something that had come up in conversation. This boy just saw Aaron as a funny, quirky kid who just did what he did, and accepted him for the way that he was.

Aaron is now 14 years old and in his second year of secondary school, and I think he has a good understanding of his autism. I'm sure he will have plenty of other questions in the future, and I will do my best to answer them when the time comes, but right now he is happy going to school, watching YouTube, taking drama classes and playing on his game console – things you could find any 14-year-old doing.

Chapter 8

THE 'AUTISM TALK'

In this chapter, I would like to share with you some stories from the wonderful families whom I work with, to give you an idea of the different ways the 'Autism Talk' can be approached. Each of the families has given me permission to write about them (with their names changed to protect their privacy). Remember, when and how you tell your child about their diagnosis is a personal decision, but these stories will, I hope, help you find a path that is right for you.

Telling a child immediately after the diagnostic process

GEMMA, 9 YEARS OLD, ASPERGER SYNDROME

Gemma was 9 years old when she went through the assessment process for autism. Her twin brother, Josh, was diagnosed with Asperger syndrome when he was in preschool. Josh was made aware of his diagnosis in early primary school through reading the book *All Cats Have Asperger Syndrome* by Kathy Hoopmann and talking to his parents about how he was like the cat. I had worked with

Josh for about 12 months prior to working with Gemma, so she was familiar with me and was happy to come and see me for several sessions before we started the diagnostic assessment.

During the assessment process, Gemma mentioned to her parents that she thought she was being 'tested' and was curious as to why. Once the diagnostic assessment was complete, and I had spoken to Gemma's parents about her having autism, Gemma's parents asked if I could help them talk to her about her diagnosis.

Gemma came in for her next session with her mother and father. I talked to her about the special things we had done over the previous few weeks and said that I wanted to explain what we had learned.

To start with, I asked Gemma to make a list of all the things she was good at. Her parents helped her come up with some ideas too. Then we talked about things that were challenges for her, and we listed them on the other side of the page.

Once we had a list of things on both sides of the page, we talked about the fact that everyone has different things they are good at and things they are challenged by, and that we can use our strengths to help overcome our challenges. We worked through Gemma's lists and thought of ways that she could use her strengths to help with her challenges. For example, Gemma identified one of her strengths as telling jokes and making people laugh, and a challenge for her was making friends. We talked about how she might be able to use her skills in making people laugh to connect with others and help her make friends.

Then I talked to Gemma about her pattern of strengths and challenges and let her know that there are other children who have a similar pattern to her. We then gave that pattern a name – autism or Asperger's. Given that Gemma's brother is also on the spectrum, it was easiest for her to understand the term Asperger's as relating to her, so that is the name we decided to use.

After talking to Gemma about Asperger syndrome, and what that meant for her, we discussed the fact that her Asperger's was only a part of who she is, and there were many other things that made her 'Gemma.' I introduced the idea of Gemma being her 'label' and Asperger's being one of her many 'ingredients.' We then made a poster of all the qualities that made her who she is and Gemma chose a photo of herself to be added to the poster so they could put it up at home.

Gemma's parents then asked some questions to help Gemma understand more about Asperger's. We talked about her brain working differently to that of some other children, and that different thinking could be a really good thing. We also let her know that there are lots of other girls like her with Asperger's and autism.

Gemma left the session appearing happy and comfortable with the new information she had gained about herself, and knowing that we could talk more about it at any time she wanted to.

Telling a child to help them understand their behavior better

TOM, 7 YEARS OLD, AUTISM SPECTRUM DISORDER AND MILD INTELLECTUAL DISABILITY

Tom received a diagnosis of autism and intellectual disability at the age of 5 years, just prior to commencing school. However, his mother did not speak to him about his diagnosis straightaway.

When Tom was around 7 years old, he came home distressed after an incident at school in which he had reacted in an inappropriate way. There had been a number of incidents in the weeks prior that had left him feeling confused and upset, and on this day, he started to talk to his mother about what had happened, while he was relaxing in the bath. Tom's mother took this opportunity to talk to Tom about his thoughts and feelings during negative experiences at school, and asked him whether he sometimes felt confused or didn't know how to react to situations, even though he knew he should be doing something. Tom agreed that what his mother described was exactly how he felt, and that he often didn't know what to do or say when something happened. At this point, Tom's mother asked him if he had heard about autism, and he said he had. It was then explained to Tom that he had autism and this meant that his brain thought about situations differently. Tom's mother also reassured him that he could learn ways to help his brain work the right way for him and react in more appropriate ways.

After having autism explained to him, Tom was visibly relieved, and asked lots of questions to make sense of what autism meant for him – for example: "Is that why I don't understand the rules of tag at lunch time?"

Now several years older, Tom has accepted his diagnosis and feels like it helps him to be better understood. His parents are also able to use autism as a framework to have open discussions about difficult situations, explore Tom's point of view, and talk about things that could have been done to resolve the situation or improve the outcome.

Telling a child as they are becoming aware of differences

SOPHIE, 7 YEARS OLD, AUTISM SPECTRUM DISORDER

Sophie was first diagnosed with autism spectrum disorder when she was 4 years old. She received support from early childhood intervention services, as well as attending regular sessions with a speech pathologist and psychologist, from the time of her diagnosis.

Sophie's family had not spoken to her specifically about autism. However, Sophie was aware that she needed help with things such as managing her emotions and expressing herself clearly with words.

When Sophie was approaching the end of Grade 1 – her second year of primary school – she began talking to her parents about some things that were hard for her at school and why she was different to her peers. They decided it was time to tell Sophie about her autism, and asked me to help them discuss her diagnosis with her at our next session.

Prior to the session, Sophie and her mother read *Me and My Brain: Ellie's Story* by Antoniette Preston and Kerryn Lisa, which introduces a girl with autism and the things she does differently and finds challenging. Sophie related to the girl in the story and could see that she was similar.

The next day, Sophie's father came with her to my clinic to participate in the session. We talked about all the great things about Sophie and made a list of her strengths and challenges. Then we discussed how she could use her strengths to overcome her challenges, and that the pattern of things she is good at and things she finds difficult is similar to that of some other children, and the name for the pattern is 'autism.'

Sophie accepted this well, and mentioned that the girl in the story that she read the night before, Ellie, had autism too. We then talked about how there were many girls and boys who have autism, just like her.

Sophie was given an opportunity to ask some questions at this time, but she didn't have anything she wanted to ask. We then played an 'I Spy' board game together, and used Sophie's skill at finding things in the game to illustrate how her autism and attention to detail, which was one of her strengths, could help her do lots of things.

Since our initial discussion, Sophie has had several other conversations with her parents about her autism and other children she knows at school who have autism, and appears to be comfortable with what autism means for her.

Telling a child in a gradual way following diagnosis

MATT, 10 YEARS OLD, ASPERGER SYNDROME

Following completion of the diagnostic process at the age of 10 years, Matt's mother decided to introduce Matt to the idea that he had Asperger syndrome in a gradual way over several months. Matt already knew he was different, commenting to his mother that sometimes he "felt like an alien" at school. Matt's mother wanted him to learn about his diagnosis in a way that was positive, rather than him thinking something was wrong with him.

Initially, Matt's diagnosis was spoken about in general terms. Matt's mother talked to him about visiting his psychologist to have a better understanding of how his brain worked, and discussed his various strengths and challenges. Then, after a few months, they discussed how all of those things together meant that Matt had something called 'Asperger syndrome.'

Since then, Matt and his mother have discussed what Asperger's means for him in his everyday life. They talk about how sometimes Matt sees things differently and how that can be challenging, and they also talk about his great memory and intelligence. Now in secondary school, Matt understands that he sometimes sees things differently to his peers and has different needs, and he is alright with that.

Talking about autism from day one

BEN, 2 YEARS OLD, AUTISM SPECTRUM DISORDER AND MODERATE INTELLECTUAL DISABILITY

Ben was diagnosed with autism at the age of 2 years, and his parents started talking about autism as an everyday part of their life from that point on. They used Ben's autism to explain why he was going to appointments, and to help his sisters understand some of his behavior.

Although autism had been talked about openly in his home most of his life, it was not until Ben was around 9 years old that he started asking questions about his diagnosis. His reading skills had been developing well, and one day Ben read on the sign at his school that it was 'autism specific.' He first asked his older sister, Jenny, what 'specific' meant, and after she gave him a definition, he asked what 'autism' was. Jenny explained autism to Ben in simple terms, and that was the end of the discussion.

Later that year, on Christmas Day, Ben and his family were driving to visit relatives when he again asked what autism is. Ben's parents took the opportunity to explain further that having autism meant Ben's brain worked differently to someone without autism, and that his thoughts and perceptions of the world were different and unique because of his autism. They also talked about Ben's strengths and that there were things he needed extra support with, such as his communication skills, or help to calm down when he was anxious or stressed.

As they talked, Ben asked each of his family members in turn if they had autism, which they don't. Ben then asked about the children at his special school and the mainstream school he was attending part-time. His mother told him that all the children at his special school had autism just like him, and that there were some children at his mainstream school who had autism, but most of the kids did not. That seemed to be enough information for Ben at that time and the conversation ended.

Ben's family continues to talk openly to him about his autism and answer his questions whenever they arise.

Receiving an autism diagnosis as a teenager

EMMA, 15 YEARS OLD, ASPERGER SYNDROME

Emma underwent assessment for autism at the age of 15, as she had a history of mild social difficulties and learning problems, and her parents felt she might meet the criteria for a diagnosis. With a diagnosis, additional support could be arranged at school that could assist her as she moved into her senior years.

In a meeting with her pediatrician and parents, Emma was told that the results of the assessment meant she had Asperger syndrome. Emma said she was a bit shocked to be told she had Asperger's, but didn't really feel positive or negative about it at the time.

Emma told me that she had always felt a bit different, and following her diagnosis, she was able to reflect on her experiences in primary school. She recognized that she had more social difficulties when she was younger, and was probably bullied because other kids must have been able to see that and chose to target her because of it.

Thankfully, now in secondary school, she has a good group of friends. Emma told her close friends about her diagnosis. She said that they were accepting and supportive, and really didn't see her any differently than before.

Overall, Emma said she is glad she knows about her Asperger's, as it has helped her receive the extra support she needs at school and has helped her to better understand herself, but there are days she thinks it would be easier if she didn't have it at all.

Chapter 9

TROUBLESHOOTING

As a parent about to tell your child they have autism, it is natural to have concerns.

Regardless of how well you plan what you are going to say, and choose the best possible time to start a conversation, there are no guarantees around how your child will react to being told about their diagnosis. Some children might be relieved to have a reason for their differences, or just accept it as not a big deal, but others may be upset about being different or want to know how to make it go away.

While many children will react in a positive way to being told they have autism, it is also important to consider that a negative reaction could happen at the time your child is told about their diagnosis or at another time in their life when they are more aware of their differences or challenges.

On the following pages, you will find common concerns raised by parents regarding their child's reaction to being told they have autism, and some practical strategies to manage these situations effectively if they do occur.

What do I do if my child uses their diagnosis as an excuse?

Having a child who uses their autism as an excuse is a very common concern for parents, and a problem that can arise at any point in a child's journey. I think it occurs because children with autism can see that sometimes others get out of doing challenging things because of a difficulty they have, and so they think that perhaps they can use their autism as an excuse to get out of doing things that make them uncomfortable.

What we need to do as parents is to reinforce that having autism doesn't mean you can't do things that others can do; it just means that sometimes you might need some help. We can do this by teaching children self-help strategies and modeling how to problem-solve. For example, if your child says they can't do something because they have autism, you might say, "I understand this is hard for you because of your autism, so what can I do to help you? Let's think about how to manage this situation in a better way." It helps to point out your child's capabilities and how they can use them, so they are not getting stuck thinking about all the things that they can't do or have trouble with.

It is also important not to provide excuses for your child. Yes, they have autism, and yes, that can make it difficult for them to regulate their emotions and behavior, but autism is a reason, not an excuse. If your child hears you excuse their inappropriate behavior by saying to someone that they can't help it because they have autism, or that they won't be able to do something because of their diagnosis, the message they will get from you is that their autism means they don't have to be responsible for their behavior and that they are less able than their peers. Instead, you can acknowledge that autism contributes to your child's behavior, and talk about what you are doing to assist your child to manage situations more appropriately. For example, if your child hits another child in the playground, you could say to the child and parent, "I'm very sorry that Johnny hit you. That was not okay. He has autism and sometimes he finds it hard to manage his frustration. We are working on helping him use his words instead of hitting." In this way you are using autism to explain the reason for the child's behavior, but you are also acknowledging that it was not appropriate and that they can change their behavior with the right support.

The message that we really want our children to hear is that while their autism can mean they have challenges, we can work together to help them develop their skills and accommodate their needs.

What do I do if my child is worried about being different?

Most children go through stages of worrying about being different. It may be because they wear glasses, because they have curly hair, or even because they have a smelly sandwich for lunch every day. When a child is told they have autism, they are being told they are different not just in what they wear or how they might look, but in how their brain works, and this can be a source of concern for them.

As a parent, you can support your child's concerns about being different by highlighting the fact that everyone has differences that make them unique, and those differences should be celebrated. While having autism means a child might think differently to some of their neurotypical peers, it also means they think in similar ways to other children with autism. And while there is a name for the particular pattern of strengths and challenges that your child has, everyone has strengths and challenges that make them a little different. You can illustrate this by talking about similarities and differences between your child and family members and friends. Your child might be good at sport and one of their friends might also be good at sport, while another friend might struggle with sport but be really good at math. These similarities and differences don't make anyone better or worse than anyone else – they make them individuals.

If your child feels that their differences make it hard for them to connect with others, it can be helpful to find a support group or an interest group that will link your child to other kids like them. For example, many autism support organizations around the world run social groups for children, adolescents and adults with autism, to give autistic individuals an opportunity to meet and develop friendships with other people on the spectrum. Alternatively, your child's special interests could give them a link to others in the community with similar interests and ideas. For example, my son Aaron has joined a local model railway club, which he attends once a month. It gives him an opportunity to be with others who like trains as much as he does and feel like he has somewhere he belongs. I also have many clients who have joined sporting clubs, coding clubs, LEGO® clubs, dance or art classes that have given them a chance to be a part of the community and relate to others around their common interest.

For some children, it is the difference in how they relate to people and manage situations that causes them to worry. If this is the case for your child, and they are worried because they have noticed that they struggle with having conversations with their friends or managing their emotions appropriately, and they feel that others are aware of these differences too, it can be helpful to seek support to develop their skills in these areas. For example, you might involve your child in a social skills group with other kids who have difficulties with the same things. This can help your child see that there are other kids who have the same challenges as them, and they can learn strategies together. You can also work with your child to identify specific situations that are challenging for them, and help them overcome their difficulties in those situations by brainstorming ideas about what to say and do, and practicing how they might react or respond.

What do I do if my child doesn't understand what it means to have autism?

Even when you have tried to tailor information to your child's developmental level, and think you have explained autism in a clear and simple way, some children will just not be able to grasp the idea that the word 'autism' applies to them, or will give no indication that they understand what you have told them.

If this happens to you, don't be discouraged. It may be that your child is not quite ready to relate what you have said to who they are, or that the concepts you have introduced are still too abstract for them to understand. What it does mean, however, is that you have started the conversation, and you can take some time to think about how to continue this journey in whatever way you feel will work best for you and your child.

You might choose to continue to incidentally point out strengths and challenges in your child and others to help them understand and accept their differences, or help them see that they sometimes see things differently in their everyday life, and then move on to supporting them to understand autism further when they're a little bit older and more receptive to it.

You might choose to leave it for a while and not mention autism again until another opportunity arises and you feel your child will have a better understanding of the concepts you are introducing.

You might try to illustrate autism in a different way by finding a character in a book, TV show or movie that is similar to your child, and relating the qualities that the character demonstrates to autism. This might help them better understand why 'autism' describes them and their behavior.

Remember that a deeper understanding of autism will develop over time, so if your child doesn't understand initially, that doesn't mean they are never going to understand. Their understanding is going to grow and their idea of how autism impacts them is going to change as they develop.

What do I do if my child does not accept their diagnosis?

While in my experience it does not happen very often, it is understandable that for some children, finding out they have autism is not welcome news.

They may think that it means they are 'sick' or inferior in some way. They may be worried that if anyone finds out, they will lose their friends. They may not agree that they are different, and not want to see themselves as anything other than the same as their peers. They might also find it difficult to accept their diagnosis if they have a sibling or peer with autism who presents very differently to them. Particularly for children who have worked very hard to 'fit in' for years, being told they are in fact different to their friends can sometimes be devastating.

If your child does react in a negative way to their diagnosis, the best thing we can do as parents is to reassure them and provide them with reliable information. Let them know that autism describes a difference in brain function that is not bad or scary; it's just different. Also make sure they know that they are not alone and that there are many people at their school and in their community who have autism too.

As I have said before, autism is only a part of who a person is, so if your child chooses not to identify as autistic because it doesn't fit the current picture of who they are, that is alright.

It is also important to respect your child's wishes regarding who is told about their diagnosis. If they do not want you to share it with anyone, you should respect that. If you feel it is necessary to share the information with health professionals or teachers, talk to your child about this and help them understand why these people need to know.

In the rare case where you feel your child's behavior or moods have changed in a negative way following them finding out about their diagnosis, it can be a good idea to seek some professional help from a psychologist, social worker or counselor. Providing your child with the opportunity to speak to someone who understands autism and the feelings they are experiencing regarding their diagnosis can make a big difference to their wellbeing and help them on their journey to acceptance.

One of my clients, Jess, had a very rocky start to her relationship with autism, and her story is a good example of how families and professionals can work together to support a child through their journey. Jess first came to see me at the age of 11 when she was in her last year of primary school.

She had gone through the diagnostic process the year before and was told about her autism, but was not convinced that the diagnosis was correct. Jess also experienced high levels of anxiety, which was being managed through a combination of medication and psychological support.

Jess's mother reported that Jess was extremely emotionally volatile at home, regularly going into rages where she verbally attacked or physically hit out at her mother and younger brother. Jess was also struggling socially at school, and had a difficult relationship with her teacher, resulting in her being resistant to attend school and elevating her levels of anxiety. Jess's parents felt that while Jess's behavior had been challenging before her diagnosis, it had deteriorated over the weeks and months following, and they were concerned about the impact it was having on her wellbeing and behavior. I worked with Jess and her family to support Jess to better manage her emotions at home, as well as helping to reduce her anxiety and increase her understanding of social situations, and she made great progress over several months.

Unfortunately, as we approached Jess's last few months in Grade 6, the difficulties at school came to a head and Jess's parents made the decision to move her and her brother to another school. Jess was happy about this move as she had friends at the new school from her netball team. However, she still found the transition difficult, and struggled to find her place with a new social structure to navigate. Around this time, Jess told me that she didn't like who she was and felt like she could never change. She also said she had often thought about hurting herself when she was upset or in a rage. Jess was, however, willing to work with me to help her feel better about herself and find better ways of managing the challenges she was facing.

With the support of myself, Jess's family, and her pediatrician, we worked on helping Jess feel more positive about herself, her abilities and her autism. This support included helping Jess develop further skills in navigating social situations and friendships, building her self-esteem and self-worth, helping Jess understand what autism means for her and that she is not alone, and building effective strategies for Jess to manage her anxiety and emotions.

Jess is now doing well in her first year of secondary school, and has a much better outlook on life and her abilities. Obviously, there are days when things are hard to manage, or when her emotions get the better of her, but her journey is a much more positive one, and she has the support in place to help her through any future challenges that arise along the way.

I think the most important thing to remember as a parent, regardless of how your child reacts to learning about their diagnosis, is that you are not alone. There is support available if you need it. Talking to other parents who have children with autism, and professionals who are experienced in working with families like yours, will give you the support and strategies you need to help you and your child navigate this journey together.

PART 2

TELLING OTHERS ABOUT YOUR CHILD'S AUTISM DIAGNOSIS

Chapter 10

WHY SHOULD I SHARE MY CHILD'S DIAGNOSIS WITH OTHERS?

Making the decision to tell others about your child's autism can be an emotional and confronting process. To tell others, you first need to have accepted the diagnosis yourself, and that can be difficult for many parents. Telling others also seems to make the diagnosis more 'real,' as it means it is no longer something that just you or your family knows, and that can feel like a really big step.

It is also important to consider the wishes of your child when deciding who needs to know about their diagnosis. Depending on their age and understanding, they may have very definite ideas about who should know and who shouldn't, and you may need to discuss why it is necessary to tell some people, while also trying to respect their need for privacy.

Although it can be a difficult decision to make, telling the important people in your child's life about their autism diagnosis can make a positive difference not only to your child, but to those caring for them as well.

When deciding who to tell about your child's autism, and what information to share, it is helpful to think about why you are sharing the diagnosis. What purpose will telling others about your child's autism serve? Some common reasons for sharing a child's diagnosis are discussed in detail below.

Increased understanding

One reason families have for sharing their child's diagnosis is to increase other people's understanding of their child and their behavior. In fact, in my own life, and in the lives of many of the families I work with, this would have to be one of the most common reasons for letting others know a child has autism.

As autism is an 'invisible' condition, it may not be evident to others when they first meet your child that they can have difficulty with their communication, emotional regulation, sensory processing or behavior. Children who are more severely affected by their autism are likely to have needs that are essential to communicate to a carer from the start, whereas children with more mild autistic characteristics may not have obvious needs and may have learned strategies to manage in challenging situations. While you might think it would be good not to mention autism and wait and see how your child fares in a new situation, this can backfire when, after appearing to be managing well the first few times they attend, your child has a meltdown or acts out, and the carers are at a loss as to why it happened or what to do. Assumptions might then be made about your child and his or her behavior that are inaccurate or misguided, and may lead to inappropriate management of the situation.

A great illustration of this is a delightful 10-year-old boy with Asperger's called Jonathon, whom I see regularly at my practice. Jonathon is very intelligent and has great language skills. However, his natural tone of voice and volume can come across as harsh and a bit aggressive. While Jonathon is working on adapting how he speaks to be more socially acceptable, he often needs prompting to remember to do this. Teachers at Jonathon's school who know him well are aware that he has Asperger's and that he has difficulty regulating his tone and volume, and are accepting of this. Unfortunately, there have been staff in the past who were unfamiliar with Jonathon and did not know about his difficulties, who have interpreted his way of speaking as rude and argumentative, and punished him for how he has spoken to them. This has inevitably led to Jonathon becoming distressed and having meltdowns, as he has not understood what he has done wrong or why he has been punished. In this case, the understanding and acceptance of Jonathon's behavior by his teachers has occurred through their knowledge of his diagnosis, and has made a positive difference to his experience at school.

Being open about your child's autism from the start allows those people caring for your child to be equipped to manage challenging situations that may occur, as well as having a better understanding of the reasons behind your child's behavior. With this understanding, it is more likely that your child will be accepted for who they are, rather than have the adults caring for them trying to make them meet an unrealistic ideal, and punishing them when they fail to fit the norm.

It is also good to remember that promoting understanding and acceptance of your child with autism through sharing their diagnosis does not have to be limited to adults, but can be targeted at peers and siblings as well. Sometimes when an autistic child engages in behaviors that are unusual or aggressive, other children may become fearful or label the child as 'naughty.' Being able to explain the child's difficulties and why they are behaving in a particular way, in terms that peers or siblings can relate to, can again support understanding and acceptance of the child. And it is amazing how accepting children can be when they are given the right information.

An example that comes to mind is of a young child with autism who was attending a local childcare center. This boy was about 4 years old and nonverbal. He was also very clumsy, often bumping into things and knocking down toys and equipment unintentionally. Some other children at the center were becoming increasingly annoyed at this boy for knocking into them or destroying their block constructions, so one of the teachers spoke to the children about the fact that this boy's legs and body didn't work the same way their bodies did, so sometimes he tripped over or knocked into things, and he didn't mean to do it. She also told them he was getting some help so he would not trip and knock into things as much. The following week, this child again walked through a group of children on the mat and knocked down some construction. As one of the boys started to get angry, another said, "It's okay. His legs don't work like ours and he knocks things over sometimes. He didn't mean it."

I feel that by sharing information about your child's diagnosis with those involved with your child, you can promote understanding not just of your child's behaviors but of autism in general, and when there is better understanding, it is hoped that acceptance will follow.

Support and accommodations

Most children with autism require some level of support to assist them to participate and achieve at home, at preschool or school, and out in the community. To receive this support and have accommodations made for them, others need to know what the child needs and why. In these situations, it is not just about sharing your child's diagnosis, but also sharing information about their individual needs so that supports can be tailored specifically for them.

To receive the right support, it is not enough just to say that your child has autism. While there are many accommodations that are considered helpful to most children with autism, such as using visuals to support communication and reduce anxiety, autistic children are so unique and individual that specific information is needed to create a picture of what your child's autism means for them, and what they need to help them succeed. With this information, organizations and individuals can put supports in place to help your child participate and achieve in any environment.

This becomes particularly important when your child is being cared for by others for extended periods such as preschool or school, childcare, and extracurricular activities. While it is likely that you as a parent automatically put supports in place to help your child, others will not know what to do unless you specifically tell them. For example, you might always ensure that the different kinds of food on your child's plate do not touch, because you know this causes them stress. Or you know that you have to phrase questions in a certain way for your child to understand them. But what happens if you have not told childcare about these accommodations? Without this information, your child may become distressed in a situation that could have been easily avoided if the carers had known more about your child's needs.

Sharing information about your child's diagnosis, and how best to care for them, will assist teachers and carers to create the best possible environment for your child to participate and learn to their full potential.

Access to services and funding

While it is helpful to share a child's diagnosis to promote understanding and have appropriate support in place, it is also important to note that many organizations will only offer support for children who have an autism diagnosis or another diagnosed disability. In these cases, sharing your child's diagnosis is essential to getting them the support that they need.

Some services and funding bodies will require proof of your child's diagnosis, usually from a pediatrician, psychologist and a speech pathologist. In addition to the diagnosis, other services may require information regarding what your child needs support with, how their difficulties impact on your family, and the results of assessments that measure your child's skills in different areas such as speech, reasoning skills and adaptive behavior (e.g. social skills, fine and gross motor development, independence skills, etc.).

The process of sharing your child's diagnosis for funding can be a challenging one as it often requires you to look at all the negatives in your situation to make a case for your need for support. As parents, we are used to trying to find positives and celebrating achievements, however small, so having to look at everything that is not working and that is a struggle for your child, and having to explain these difficulties to others, can be extremely confronting. If you are required to go through this process at any point, try to see it as a means to an end, and focus on the benefits the supports will give you, rather than on the negatives.

Educating others

While some of the parents I work with prefer to share their child's diagnosis only on a 'need to know' basis, others feel that they have an opportunity to educate the wider community by sharing their child's diagnosis with anyone who is interested or may benefit from knowing.

This is very much a personal choice and depends not just on the person but also on the situation they are in.

One way parents may choose to educate others is to use 'alert cards' that explain their child's diagnosis and behavior. Organizations like the National Autism Association (United States) and the National Autistic Society (United Kingdom) produce these cards, or parents can create their own, and they can be handed to people to explain an autistic child's behavior when the opportunity arises or when they can't find the words.

Alternatively, parents may openly discuss their child's diagnosis with others at preschool or school, or when out in the community, to explain their child's behavior and help others understand autism more fully.

Whatever your reason, sharing your child's diagnosis and their journey with others can make a difference not just to your child's life, but also to the autistic community as a whole.

Chapter 11

COMMON CONCERNS OF PARENTS

Many parents have concerns about telling others about their child's autism diagnosis. For some, it is about the reaction of family and friends. For others, it is the impact that telling others might have on how their child is treated or how they might be judged themselves. And of course, for many it is 'all of the above.'

While in a perfect world these concerns would be unfounded, the reality is that parents may be faced with situations in which news of their child's diagnosis is not received in the way they hoped. However, I believe that the benefits of telling the important people in your child's life about their diagnosis far outweigh any negative reactions that may occur.

The misinformation associated with autism

In recent years, autism has become more widely accepted and better understood in the general population. However, many feel that misinformation around autism still exists amongst individuals and within some communities and this can impact on a parent's decision to share their child's diagnosis with others. Because of this misinformation, assumptions are made about people with autism, not based on fact, but on outdated theories, isolated personal experience with an individual with autism, or something a person has seen in a movie or on TV. When a person's only knowledge of autism comes from watching *Rainman* or *Mercury Rising*, it can be hard for them to see that people with autism are individuals who are as different to each other as they are similar. With more accurate portrayals of individuals with autism in the media, and more real and varied autistic voices being heard across the world, understanding and acceptance of autism improves every day.

While the stories I hear from families about sharing their child's diagnosis are predominantly positive, some families do report experiencing isolation and exclusion as a result of making their child's autism known amongst family and friends. An example of this is an unfortunate situation that the parents of one of my clients found themselves in at a school picnic. Sarah, 9 years old, had recently received a diagnosis of Asperger syndrome, and was very accepting of her diagnosis. She had a few friends at school, but one in particular who was also a bit 'quirky,' whom Sarah liked to play with. After Sarah was diagnosed, her mother saw her friend's mother at school and thought she would take the opportunity to let her know that Sarah had Asperger's. Sarah's mother expected this other mother to be understanding, as their children had been friends for several years, but she responded in quite a cold manner. Then several weeks later at a school picnic, Sarah's mother observed this parent calling her daughter away from Sarah whenever she went to play with her. As upsetting as this was for Sarah's mother, Sarah herself did not really notice, and sought out other children to play with. In contrast, another friend of

Sarah's and her family have made more effort to invite Sarah to playdates and include her in activities since they were told about her diagnosis.

I think that the important thing to take away from this story is that though there will always be ignorant or unaccepting people in the world, they appear to be far outnumbered by people who are welcoming, understanding and supportive, and these are the people we want to be in our lives and sharing our journeys.

Giving a label for life

Every now and then I have a parent who comes to me asking whether a diagnosis of autism can be reversed in the future, and concerned about the impact of telling others their child has autism when it may not be the case when they are older. This is a valid question, and one that I think comes from a place of hope for their child's future, but also suggests that they are still developing an understanding of what autism is.

In response to these concerns, I find it best to go back to explaining the neurological basis for autism. As I discussed in Chapter 2, autism is a neurodevelopmental disorder, and as such is characterized by differences in the way the brain works. These differences in brain function are demonstrated in the way a child behaves, communicates and interacts with others.

It may be argued by some that as behavior is used to diagnose autism, if a person no longer displays behaviors at a level consistent with autism, then they could lose their diagnosis, but I do not feel that this should be the case. While an individual with autism can develop ways to manage their difficulties effectively over time and may therefore appear 'less autistic,' the brain difference remains and therefore, in my opinion, so does their autism.

I believe that when it will be beneficial to the child to share their diagnosis, it is important to do so. However, as a child grows older and develops skills to manage their difficulties, they may reach a point where they no longer require additional support, and consequently they may not feel it is necessary to tell others about their diagnosis. This is very much a personal choice and will depend on the individual and what autism means to them.

Lowered expectations of the child's abilities

Another common concern for parents is that if others know that a child has autism, they will have lower expectations of what the child can do and achieve. Some parents would prefer not to tell teachers or carers about their child's diagnosis, as they do not want their child to be treated differently or have their potential limited due to assumptions being made about their abilities.

In my experience, it is the opposite that occurs. Not providing this information to those caring for a child with autism more often leads to them being limited as accommodations are not put in place to allow the child to succeed. Without knowledge of a child's difficulties and why they occur, teachers and carers are more likely to misinterpret an autistic child's behavior as naughty or disruptive, and potentially use inappropriate strategies or punishments to manage the behavior.

When accurate information is shared to give teachers and carers a clear picture of an autistic child's needs and abilities, supports can be put in place to ensure the child is given the opportunities they need to reach their potential.

How the child feels about telling others they have autism

Particularly as children get older, parents may become concerned with how their child or adolescent feels about telling others they have autism.

When children are little, parents often tell others about their child's diagnosis to ensure others understand their behavior and can support them in the best ways possible, without considering what the child may want. However, children or adolescents who know about their own diagnosis may have an opinion about who they want told, and this may conflict with what their parent feels is necessary to assist them at school or in the community.

Children may be concerned about how their friends will react if they know they have autism, worried that they might be teased or bullied, or not want to be treated differently in the classroom. These concerns may result in them not wanting anyone to know about their diagnosis.

Ultimately, you as their parent should make a decision about who to tell, based on your child's best interests, and that may not be in agreement with your child's wishes. I find that when situations like this occur, it is best to talk to the child directly about who you feel are important people to tell about the diagnosis – for example, a teacher – and why it is necessary for them to know. They should also be reassured that information about their autism is personal and private, and will not be shared with anyone else unless they want it to be shared. The child can then be given the choice as to who else, if anyone, they want told about their autism and how they want this to be done.

Receiving unsolicited advice

For some parents, wanting to share their child's diagnosis is marred by the barrage of unsolicited and usually unhelpful advice they seem to attract, sometimes from total strangers. It seems that just like when a woman is pregnant, and everyone at the local shopping center becomes an expert on child rearing and pregnancy, so too does the disclosure that your child has autism seem to bring 'experts' out of the woodwork to give their opinion about anything from what causes autism, to how to cure it, to how to discipline your child, and everything in between. Even for parents with a thick skin, there are days when an offhand comment by a parent at school about 'their cousin who cured autism by removing all technology from their home' or 'the news article about a new drug that cures autism' can be enough to open the floodgates.

However, it is important to note that many parents of typically developing children also find themselves on the receiving end of unsolicited advice at some stage during their journey, and it is not a reflection on them or their children. Rather, it is a reflection on the adult who thinks they have the right to comment on another person's situation and behavior. Regardless of whether they are offering a suggestion because they want to help, or are commenting because they think they know it all, these people do not know your situation or your story, and as such, do not deserve or command your attention.

At times when unsolicited advice or comments really seem to hit a nerve, I find it good to remember that you are the expert on your child. What others think about you or your child really isn't important. You know what you need to do to support your child and how to do it, and you are doing the best you can.

Being judged

Being a parent is hard work, and it is made harder for some by the feeling that they are judged for their parenting decisions and for their children's behavior. They may feel judged by others for what they are putting into their bodies while pregnant, for how or what their child is fed, or for how they manage their child's behavior. When your child is diagnosed with autism, it can seem like another opportunity for judgment. And not just from others, but from yourself too.

For some parents, finding out their child has autism makes them second guess everything they have done up until that point. Did they do something wrong during the pregnancy? Did their postnatal depression cause their child to develop autism? Has their parenting style contributed to their child's symptoms? And although they have probably been told many times that they have done nothing to cause their child's autism, some doubt may still remain. With that doubt can come a reluctance to talk to others about their child's diagnosis, due to concerns that others may suspect the parent had a role in the development of their child's autism.

While there may still be individuals in the community who do not understand autism, and a lot of questions remain regarding how and why it develops, most experts agree that there is no single cause of autism and no specific actions by a parent during pregnancy or early childhood that can make a child autistic. If we as parents can remember these facts, and try to put our doubts and the comments of misinformed individuals aside, we can feel confident that those we choose to tell about our child's diagnosis will be supportive rather than judgmental.

Chapter 12

WHO SHOULD YOU TELL ABOUT YOUR CHILD'S DIAGNOSIS?

When a child receives a diagnosis of autism, it can have an impact not only on the child, but on family, friends and the wider community. Parents often need to consider who they should share their child's diagnosis with not only to better support their child but also to gain support themselves. There are many factors that may influence your decision about who to tell, including how close the person is to you and your child, their role in your child's life, and their capacity to understand and accept your child's diagnosis.

Extended family

Family members such as grandparents can be a great source of support when a child is diagnosed with autism. However, it is important to remember that while many family members will be supportive, others may have difficulty understanding and accepting the diagnosis, and this is likely to impact on whether you choose to share your child's diagnosis with them or not.

Grandparents may experience grief and a sense of loss similar to that experienced by some parents when they find out their grandchild has autism. In addition to this, grandparents may also experience a sense of sadness and sorrow for what their own child (the parent) is going through. While some grandparents may want to understand as much as they can about autism and get involved in supporting their grandchild, others may insist there is 'nothing wrong' and be resistant to taking on strategies to help them. When the latter is the case, it does not necessarily mean that the grandparent doesn't care, but instead it may indicate that they are not able or not ready to see the difference in their grandchild that others have identified and named. Acceptance of a child's diagnosis by a grandparent or family member may come eventually, but it may also be something that they never agree with and are resistant to acknowledge.

For the majority of families I work with, extended family members such as grandparents play a very important role in the care of children with autism. With grandparents often caring for their grandchildren on a regular basis, they have the opportunity to attend therapy sessions, speak to teachers and carers and get involved in supporting children with autism at home. Grandparents are often also able to provide parents with a break from their caring role to spend time with typically developing siblings, or for the parents to invest time in their own relationship.

I was lucky to have parents who were accepting of my son Aaron's diagnosis from the beginning, and were open to using strategies to support him with his communication and behavior. They also helped me by allowing me to talk openly about the challenges I was facing with him and gave me a break every now and then to give me time to recharge and care for myself. While my parents were able to give me the support that I needed, I know that this is not always the case.

When a grandparent or other family member is unable or unwilling to accept a child's diagnosis of autism, it can sometimes place a strain on family relationships. If this occurs, some parents may choose to distance themselves from the family members who are unable to support them in their journey, while others may choose to make a change to their relationship. This change might involve choosing not to discuss autism with the family member, but remaining connected in other ways.

There are also situations in which parents may make a deliberate choice not to tell other family members about their child's diagnosis. I have most often found this to be the case due to cultural or religious reasons, in which parents are aware that family members have a very negative view of any disability, including autism, due to their beliefs and would exclude the child with autism if they knew about the diagnosis. For these families, seeking external support is extremely important.

Friends

As the saying goes, "You can choose your friends, but you can't choose your family." This can become very important when parents have limited support from their family in relation to their child with autism. Even when parents do have close family ties, having people to talk to outside the family can provide unique opportunities for support and guidance that are essential to a parent's wellbeing.

When considering telling friends about a child's diagnosis, it is important to recognize that friendships can have different qualities and meet different needs. You may have friends who you know will listen to the challenges and the successes you experience without judgment and offer support when needed. You may also have other friends who do not really understand autism and so you don't talk about your children with them, focusing more on other aspects of life and common interests. While it is obviously beneficial to have supportive friends to help you through your challenges and celebrate successes with you, it may also be a relief to have someone in your life who is just interested in you and who doesn't get involved with your autism journey. That doesn't mean you shouldn't tell a friend your child has autism if you want to, but it does mean that it is okay to have friendships that are separate from your family situation and allow you just to be yourself.

Unfortunately, telling friends about your child's diagnosis can result in the loss of some people you thought were your friends. Many parents I speak to have explained that after their child's diagnosis, they had some friends who became distant and disappeared, some they chose to cut ties with, and other friends who remained strong and supportive. In addition, their child having autism provided them with the opportunity to meet new people who were on similar journeys, and make new friends who really understand. I have also found that some friends may try too hard to support you by offering advice and trying to fix things when you tell them about your situation. If what you need from a friend is just to listen, or to escape for a while, let them know that. A true friend will understand and will try to give you what you need.

Siblings

Telling a child about their brother or sister's autism diagnosis can be a big decision. As a sibling is a permanent fixture in an autistic child's life, the time you might choose to tell them is likely to vary depending on a number of factors. When thinking about telling a sibling about their brother or sister's diagnosis, it is important to consider the age of the sibling and their level of understanding, whether the sibling has noticed any differences between themselves and their brother or sister, whether the child with autism knows about their own diagnosis, and who else has been told.

If the child with autism has not been told about their diagnosis, it may be better not to explain their difficulties to a sibling using the word 'autism' but rather in terms of describing the difficulties that are most obvious. For example, when talking to a sibling about their nonverbal brother, you might tell them that "Johnny is still learning how to use his words, and sometimes it's hard for him to tell us what he wants. We can help him by getting him to choose from the pictures in his book." Alternatively, you could do an activity with the sibling that explores strengths and challenges in themselves and compare those with the strengths and challenges of their autistic brother or sister, then discuss how they can help each other with their respective challenges.

My main reasoning for not using the word 'autism' when the autistic child is not aware of their diagnosis is a simple one. While siblings invariably love each other, they do get frustrated and annoyed with each other too, and at these times they may say or do things that are not nice. What we don't want is for a sibling to use their brother or sister's diagnosis as a weapon or an insult, especially when the child doesn't know they have autism. Not only is it a very brutal way for the child to find out about their diagnosis, but they may then associate having autism with all the negative things their sibling has said about them, and this could also cause them to resent the parent for telling a sibling instead of sharing the information with them first.

When a child already knows about their autism diagnosis, I think the path to informing siblings is much more straight-forward. There are a number of books and videos aimed at different ages that explain autism from a sibling's perspective, and can provide insight into what it is like for the child with autism as well as the challenges that a sibling may face. More general books and media about autism can be useful too. (See Chapter 17 for a list of helpful books, videos and websites.)

When planning to talk to siblings, it is also important to consider their feelings and their possible reaction to finding out about their brother or sister's diagnosis. For some it might have been obvious, while for others it might be a complete surprise. Some may be embarrassed that their brother or sister has special needs, and some may be worried about their brother or sister's future or feel that they suddenly have to take on more responsibility to support and protect them. Whatever their reaction, if you have any concerns about how they are coping, it may be helpful to seek support for them to talk to someone about how they feel about their brother or sister's diagnosis and what it means to them. Many organizations also run sibling support groups that allow siblings of children with autism or other developmental disorders to come together and discuss their concerns, and connect with other young people who understand what it is like.

Teachers and carers

As I've mentioned previously, I think it is important to let teachers and carers know about your child's diagnosis and what support they need to participate effectively and get the most out of their experiences at preschool, school or out in the community. Giving teachers and carers information about your child provides the best possible opportunity for both them and the child to develop a positive relationship and have success.

Unfortunately, sometimes a teacher or carer may not agree with a child's diagnosis and therefore may not be open to supporting the child in a way a parent feels is necessary. It can be helpful to enlist the child's treating professionals to step in and advise the teacher/carer in these situations and even to provide some professional recommendations so the information is not just coming from an anxious mother or father, and cannot be so easily dismissed.

That being said, my experience with most teachers and carers is overwhelmingly positive. I have worked with countless teachers over the years who are extremely invested in making sure that all children in their care have the best possible experience and get the most out of their learning. Consequently, I feel that information not just about a child's diagnosis but also about how autism presents in them as an individual and what can be done to support them is essential to allow teachers and carers to provide the opportunities children with autism need to flourish.

Classmates

There are several situations in which I think it is really helpful to educate classmates about a child's diagnosis.

First, for children with severe behavior difficulties or intellectual disabilities, I think it can be beneficial to talk to classmates about why a child is behaving the way they are, to promote understanding and acceptance. If the child does not yet know about their diagnosis, you may choose not to use the word 'autism' but may instead describe the behaviors or difficulties the child has and what is being done to support them. It can also be good to tell classmates how they can help and what they can do if the child does something inappropriate.

For children who are aware of their own diagnosis, I think this is a situation in which you should get your child's permission to let their classmates know they have autism. If they do not want them to know, you should respect that. It can, however, be useful to let teachers know what they can say to explain a child's behavior if it becomes necessary. For example, rather than mentioning autism, it may be appropriate to tell peers that a child "is having difficulty making good choices when they are upset, and they are getting some help to learn how to manage their feelings better."

If a child does want their peers to know, it is good to have a discussion with them about what information they would like shared and how they would prefer it to be done. Some children, who want their classmates to know about their diagnosis, find it useful to talk to the class themselves to explain what autism means for them. Others may prefer a general discussion about autism by an expert before their classmates are told about their experience. Either way, this can be really empowering for the child and tends to be well received by peers as well.

Other parents

In a situation where an autistic child is behaving in ways that are inappropriate or unusual, and is likely to be coming to the attention of peers, it can be useful to explain a child's diagnosis to other parents at preschool or school. This can help to ensure there is no misinformation regarding why the child is behaving in that way, and inform others about what is being done to support the child and, if necessary, keep others safe. It also assists other parents to know what to say to their child if they come home reporting that the child with autism has done something that might be seen as 'naughty.' While there is no guarantee that all parents will be accepting of the explanation, it is my experience that most will.

A friend of mine, Cathy, has a son called Ben who has autism as well as an intellectual disability, and she recently told me about her experience when he was newly diagnosed and starting 3-year-old preschool. Cathy was still very early in her journey with autism and was not ready to let others know about her son's diagnosis. She instructed the preschool teacher to explain Ben's difficulties in terms of a language disorder if anyone asked, and under no circumstances was autism to be mentioned.

The year that followed was an incredibly difficult one for all of them. Ben was the subject of regular car park gossip as other parents speculated about what could be 'wrong' with him. He was not invited to any parties or playdates throughout the year, and he became increasingly excluded from preschool activities as he was often taken to a separate area to complete tasks rather than remaining with the group. It was a very negative experience, not just for Ben but for his whole family.

Having reflected on their challenging year, and finding herself in a different place regarding her acknowledgment of Ben's diagnosis, Cathy decided to try something different when Ben started 4-year-old preschool. Rather than hide Ben's diagnosis, Cathy created an 'All about Me' page introducing Ben and his strengths and challenges, and placed it in all the pigeon holes at the preschool so every family would receive one. The response Cathy received was overwhelmingly positive. Parents approached her to thank her for letting them know about Ben, and said that the information she had provided would help them support Ben better when they were on preschool duty. Other parents went out of their way to invite Ben to parties or arrange playdates.

Providing information about Ben's diagnosis to other parents helped all those involved with him to understand and support him, and allowed him to be included in the preschool community. The response Cathy received also gave her the confidence to continue to share Ben's diagnosis with others to promote better understanding and acceptance.

Health professionals

Particularly if the professionals in your child's team were not involved in the diagnostic process for your child, letting them know that an assessment has been completed and a diagnosis has been received is important for them to be able to do their job effectively.

It is also really important to be able to talk openly about any challenges you or your child are facing and how you are managing. If you don't feel comfortable or supported to do this with your child's therapist, whether that is a psychologist, speech pathologist, occupational therapist or doctor, it might be time for you to consider a change. For example, if you don't feel comfortable telling your child's therapist that your child is on their iPad all day because it is the only way you can get peace, or that you have to serve them chicken nuggets every night for dinner because they won't eat anything else, you may not get the level of support you need or be put in touch with other supports that might be useful because the therapist is only getting part of the story. Health professionals are there to support, not to judge, and if you are not happy with a professional you are seeing for any reason – you might not feel that they listen to you, they might not believe in the diagnosis, they might not have 'clicked' with you or your child – it is okay to look for someone else. Even if someone is supposed to be the best clinician ever, they still might not be a good fit for you or your child, and that is alright.

Finally, it is important to remember that you are in control of who you share your child's diagnosis with and how it should be done, and there are no right or wrong choices. Your opinions about who to tell may change as your child develops, but it is ultimately still your decision to make until they reach adulthood. The best thing that you can do is do what you feel is right for you and your child and be confident in that.

Chapter 13

WHAT SHOULD YOU TELL OTHERS ABOUT YOUR CHILD?

When you decide to share your child's diagnosis with others, the details you provide will depend on who you are sharing the information with and what purpose sharing your child's diagnosis will serve.

Talking to teachers and carers

For most parents, sharing their child's diagnosis to inform teachers and carers of their child's needs is something that is quite common, but there are some key pieces of information that sometimes get forgotten when the focus is on a child's need for support rather than getting to know the whole child. The following points are pieces of information that I think are important for anyone caring for your child to know: not just to manage their behavior or needs, but to be able to form a relationship with them and help them get the most out of their experiences.

LIKES AND DISLIKES

Being aware of what a child likes and doesn't like can make a big difference in creating an environment that a child is comfortable in, and can assist others with supporting them to cope with the changing demands and expectations of unfamiliar settings. Making an effort to include activities a child likes into their daily schedule, and avoiding activities they don't like where possible, can assist a child to settle into a new routine more easily. Obviously, there will be times when non-preferred activities cannot be avoided, or are necessary for a child's education, but over time children become more tolerant of these activities and are usually better able to manage them in their daily life.

SPECIAL INTERESTS

Special interests can be very powerful motivators for children with autism and are also a great way to connect with a child. They can be used to encourage participation in activities and increase a child's willingness to complete tasks, as well as supporting behavior management plans. Knowledge about special interests can also give adults caring for a child an effective and meaningful way to engage them and form a relationship with them. For example, asking a question about dinosaurs, talking about the latest development in Minecraft, or mentioning that you love My Little Pony, might instantly give a child with autism a way to connect with you, prompting interest in you and providing them an opportunity to talk about their favorite thing.

How your child communicates

It is important to know and understand how a child communicates in order to fully engage with them and meet their needs. Do they use signs to communicate, or pictures or words? If they use words, how clearly can they express themselves? Do they lose their ability to communicate with words when they are upset? Answering questions like these gives the person caring for your child the best possible opportunity to interact successfully and to be able to meet their needs when you are not there.

How best to communicate with your child effectively

Children with autism can differ greatly in their understanding of spoken language and may need supports to increase their ability to make sense of what is said to them. It is often assumed that nonverbal children must also struggle to understand language, and that children who express themselves well must have good receptive language skills. However, the opposite can also be the case. Giving those caring for your child specific information about their level of understanding, and what accommodations are needed to support how they take in and process information, is extremely important to ensure they are assisted to understand what is expected of them and what is happening in the world around them.

What your child is good at

Knowing what a child is good at or confident in can be great when trying to build a child's self-confidence and self-esteem. It can also be a helpful way of engaging a child in activities and encouraging them to work with others. A child may be really skilled with computers, so they are given the job of being 'computer monitor' to set up the computers each morning; or they might be reading at a high level, so they go to a more junior class and read a story to them once a week. For many children with autism, everyday tasks can be quite challenging, so being able to focus on strengths and help them have success with tasks at home and at school can make a big difference to their wellbeing.

WHAT YOUR CHILD STRUGGLES WITH AND HOW TO HELP

When we talk to teachers and carers about situations or activities that a child has difficulty with, it is important also to provide information about how a child can be supported. For example, if you know that your child has difficulty sitting on the mat during story time but does better when sitting on a cushion and holding a soft toy, let your child's teacher know so they can be using this strategy with your child from the beginning. As a parent, you know your child better than anyone else, so the tips and tricks you have developed to help your child manage difficult situations are useful strategies to pass on to those caring for your child.

SENSORY SENSITIVITIES

The sensory sensitivities experienced by many children with autism can have a huge impact on their ability to function in different environments. Sensitivities could involve a child's need to move constantly, aversion to noises or smells, or discomfort and irritation when wearing specific clothing. Informing teachers and carers of a child's sensitivities allows them to put processes in place to accommodate or minimize the negative impact that sensory input might have on a child and also meet a child's sensory needs. For example, if your child is very sensitive to noise, wearing headphones in class or during noisy activities such as assemblies could make a big difference in their ability to cope at school, and letting a teacher know this at the start of the year will eliminate unnecessary problems later on.

TRIGGERS

When a child is prone to becoming anxious or upset, it is very helpful to provide teachers and carers with information about the kinds of situations that are likely to trigger extreme emotional responses. Some situations may be quite common, such as when another child won't let them play or they can't have something the way they want, and other situations may be very specific to the child, such as being asked to participate in a game or being looked at in a particular way. With information about triggers, those caring for your child can put preventative measures in place to reduce the likelihood of your child becoming distressed and support your child to better regulate their emotions.

SIGNS OF STRESS

Do you recognize when your child is becoming distressed or anxious? What are the signs that alert you to your child needing support to calm down? While some children will show more obvious signs of stress such as getting out of their seat and pacing, or speaking at a louder volume, others may show more subtle signs such as playing with their hair, blinking excessively or humming. Parents often learn to recognize the ways their children demonstrate that they are stressed, and this information is extremely important to pass on to teachers and carers to help them intervene before a child gets to meltdown.

STRATEGIES FOR MANAGING CHALLENGING BEHAVIOR

Many children with autism have times when their behavior is challenging. They may have difficulty regulating their emotions, refuse to complete activities they do not like, shut down when presented with something they have not done before or become aggressive when someone excludes them in the playground. Teachers and carers will benefit from any information parents can provide about successful and effective ways to manage a child's behavior. A child may respond well to a sticker chart, a token system, activity rewards when they finish set tasks, or even just a 'high five.' Sharing your knowledge of the most effective strategies you have found to support your child's behavior will give teachers and carers the tools they need to help your child to be successful.

Siblings and classmates

When talking to siblings and classmates about your child's diagnosis, the purpose is usually to increase understanding and acceptance. With this purpose in mind, the type of information you present is likely to be different to what you share with teachers and carers. A helpful way to think about what information to share is to consider how to answer the following questions. Some sample responses have been included with each question to assist you.

WHAT IS AUTISM?

- Autism is a neurodevelopmental condition which means it is a difference in the way a person's brain works, and it is present from the time they are born.

- It is not something you can catch from others.

- Having a brain that works differently doesn't make someone a 'lesser person' – they are just different.

How are children with autism different to other children?

- Children with autism can be sensitive to things such as loud noises and how things feel to touch. They might not like to be touched by others.

- They might have difficulty talking, or they might like to talk a lot about their favorite things without listening to what others have to say.

- Some children with autism have a lot of difficulty keeping their emotions under control, so that they get upset really easily and might overreact to situations.

- It can sometimes be scary for children with autism to try new things, go somewhere new or meet new people, so they like to try to keep things the same all the time.

- Sometimes children with autism do things with their bodies that look strange. They might flap their hands, jump up and down repeatedly, rock back and forth on their chair or make funny noises with their mouths. They usually do these things when they are feeling uncomfortable to help themselves calm down.

How are children with autism similar to other children?

- Children with autism are often interested in the same kinds of things that other children are interested in. They might like sports, animals, reading, dancing, computers or LEGO®.

- They can go to school and learn new things, just like other children.

- Most children with autism want to have friends and be part of activities. They feel sad or angry if they are left out, just like other children do.

How does autism affect how children play and interact?

- Having autism often means that playing and talking to others can be difficult.

- Children with autism sometimes have difficulty looking at people's faces when they are being spoken to. It doesn't mean they are not interested in you or what you have to say; it is just hard for them to listen and look at the same time.

- Sometimes children with autism have difficulty following the rules of games, or might get stuck on playing a game their way and not want to listen to anyone else's ideas. This can make it hard for them to join in with others.

WHAT CAN YOU DO TO HELP CHILDREN WITH AUTISM?

- Help them join in your games by teaching them the rules and showing them what to do.

- Try to find a common interest to talk about together.

- Explain what is happening around them if they look uncomfortable or confused.

- Give them some extra time to respond when you talk to them. Sometimes it can be hard to think of the right words to use.

WHAT SHOULD YOU DO IF A CHILD WITH AUTISM DOES SOMETHING YOU DON'T LIKE?

- You can let a child with autism know you don't like what they are doing by clearly telling them to stop what they are doing and telling them what they can do instead.

- It is never okay for a child to hurt someone, so if a child with autism hurts you or someone around you, find an adult straightaway and get some help.

Considering questions like these can assist you to decide what information is important to share, and to present that information in a way that will be easily understood by your child's siblings and peers.

Telling extended family, friends and other parents

Extended family, friends and other parents are most likely going to need a combination of the types of information given to teachers/carers and siblings/classmates. They may need to be educated about what autism is and how it impacts your child, as well as needing information about how to support your child if they are in their care. Try to tailor the information you provide to the person you are talking to, and think about what is essential for them to know and what might not be necessary. It is also good to remember that you don't have to tell them everything all at once – let them know what you think is important for right now and you can always give them more information later if you need to.

Chapter 14

HOW SHOULD YOU SHARE YOUR CHILD'S AUTISM DIAGNOSIS?

There are many different ways you can share your child's diagnosis with others. Ultimately, the method you choose will depend on a number of factors, including who you are sharing the information with and the purpose sharing your child's diagnosis will serve.

Before you decide on how you will share your child's diagnosis, there are a few final things you need to consider.

Tailor the language to the audience

When sharing your child's diagnosis, it is important to consider who you are communicating with and what kind of language will be most appropriate and effective in getting your message across.

While the language in formal diagnostic reports might be appropriate for medical and allied health professionals, using this same language to talk to family members about autism may be confusing. The language you use is also likely to differ significantly depending on whether you are speaking to adults or children, and whether the people you are talking to are familiar with autism or not.

Thinking about how best to deliver your message to different audiences, and changing your language to suit, can make a big difference to whether the information you share is just heard or is also understood.

Provide context

Autism, at its core, is a condition that impairs social functioning, and this suggests that it should be most evident in social contexts. However, it is not that simple. Social contexts themselves are wide and varied, and an autistic child's demonstration of their difficulties is too.

While some children who are severely impacted by their autism might display characteristics in every aspect of their lives, other children with more mild presentations may only demonstrate obvious autistic traits when under pressure or in specific situations. However, just because they are not demonstrating obvious impairments, it does not mean they don't need support.

For example, your child may be very comfortable and confident in their regular classroom but struggle when they move to a specialist class or assembly. Alternatively, your child may work very well when paired with a peer for a task, but quickly becomes overwhelmed in a small group or whole-class activity.

It is necessary that others understand your child's individual presentation, and their specific needs in different contexts or environments, to ensure your child receives the support and understanding they need.

Consider how much information is necessary to share

It is important to consider the amount and types of information it is necessary to share to clearly communicate your message, and this will vary depending on your audience.

Medical and allied health professionals will often require the results of specific assessments, including clinical observations and scores, to form a clinical picture of your child and their difficulties. Schools and preschools may also need more formal diagnostic information to assist with applications for support and funding.

Alternatively, other people involved in your child's life may only want practical information about what autism means for your child and how they can best be supported, rather than becoming overwhelmed with clinical details and jargon.

A good example that comes to mind is when my son, Aaron, started school. We were applying for funding to support him with his learning, so the school required confirmation of Aaron's autism diagnosis from a speech pathologist, psychologist and pediatrician, including scores representing the severity of his autistic characteristics, his expressive and receptive language skills and his cognitive abilities. All this information was presented in several complex reports full of statistics and diagnostic terms, with very little practical information.

When I met with Aaron's teacher, Ms. Clark, for the first time, she had read the reports but had not found them at all useful, as they had not given her a picture of who Aaron was or what he could do. Ms. Clark wanted to know about

Aaron's likes and dislikes, how she could best communicate with him and help him manage being in a new environment, and anything else that I thought would be helpful. She wanted to know about him as a person, not a series of scores and diagnostic descriptions, because just knowing he had autism was not enough.

Considering the amount and type of information you share with others, depending on who they are and what their connection with your child is, will help ensure that everyone receives the information they need to support your child in the best way possible.

Consider different ways to share your child's diagnosis

As we have already discussed, there are many options for providing information to others about your child's diagnosis. The following list will give you some ideas about how to present information to suit different audiences and purposes.

PROFESSIONAL REPORTS

Professional reports are usually written by medical or allied health professionals to communicate the results of assessment, provide details of progress in therapy and make recommendations for supports.

A professional report is particularly useful when specific details regarding your child's diagnosis are required. This could be for funding applications, establishing eligibility for services or to inform a new doctor or therapist. Reports containing recommendations for supports or management strategies can also be of use to teachers and carers who need to develop plans for learning and behavior management.

The most effective professional reports are those that summarize the important findings or information in a clear way and provide practical strategies and recommendations.

OPEN LETTER

An open letter is a way to introduce your child and their diagnosis to others in a simple and relatable way. It can be a useful tool for providing information to a group of people, such as a group of families at preschool, and can be tailored specifically to an individual child including as much or as little information as a family wants to share.

The content of an open letter usually aims to inform others about a child's diagnosis, and may include details about similarities and differences to peers, behavior difficulties, and ideas about how peers can help the child with autism play and be part of activities. It can also be a great opportunity to offer to answer any questions other parents may have.

Many of the families I work with have used an open letter successfully to introduce their child to new classmates, creating an environment of understanding and acceptance amongst their peers and their peers' families.

'ALL ABOUT ME' PAGE

Another effective way to introduce your child to a teacher or classmates is to create an 'All about Me' page. An 'All about Me' page presents a summary of important information about a child and often includes a photo.

Depending on the audience, a child's 'All about Me' page may include information about a child's likes and dislikes, strengths and challenges, special interests, triggers for challenging behavior and support strategies.

A summary page of this kind can be especially useful for quick reference by replacement teachers and specialist staff, to ensure they are aware of ways to connect with the child, possible difficulties that may arise, and key support strategies to assist the child in the classroom or playground.

MEETING/DISCUSSION

Having the opportunity to speak in person to others about your child's diagnosis can be an invaluable way to clearly communicate how autism impacts your child, highlight their individual strengths and challenges, and answer questions or address concerns others may have.

Whether it is having an informal chat with family and friends about your child's autism, or formally meeting with teaching staff to discuss your child's needs, it is good to have a plan about what you want to say and what information you want to communicate. Writing down a list of important points to take with you to your discussion can make it easier to remember everything you want to say, and having copies of professional reports or recommendations on hand can be helpful when meeting with teachers and carers. It can also be beneficial to have written information about autism available to share, or links to reliable resources ready so you can direct anyone who is seeking more detailed information.

It is important to keep in mind that family and friends may need time to process the information you give them about your child, and may react in different ways. While in some situations it may be appropriate to provide a lot of information all at once, at other times you may need to share small pieces of information, and be available to answer questions when they arise.

CLASSROOM PRESENTATION

For some children with autism, telling their classmates about their diagnosis is an important step toward feeling truly accepted and understood. While some autistic children may prefer peers not to know about their diagnosis, and that should be respected, others want classmates to know about their autism to help them better understand their thinking and behavior.

There are different ways that information can be presented to a class about a child's diagnosis. Some children will want to speak to their class on their own, while others may want an adult to explain autism first before they speak, or not be present at all. If a child wants to tell their class about their diagnosis, it is important to find out how they want to share the information, and work with them to ensure the message they are trying to communicate gets through.

When an adult is going to present information to a class, they may use a variety of resources to help build an understanding of autism first, before they discuss a particular child. There are numerous toolkits and workbooks available online that provide information on how to introduce autism to children through practical activities. There are also many books and video clips publicly available that explain autism in a child-friendly and positive way. Links to some of these resources are included in Chapter 17.

Alternatively, when an autistic child wants to talk to their class, it is important that they feel supported and are encouraged by staff and students to share their story. They may choose to give a speech, do a PowerPoint presentation, or even show a video to explain their diagnosis and what autism means to them.

One of my clients, James, an 8-year-old boy with Asperger's, recently decided to talk to his class about his diagnosis while running for the Student Representative Council (SRC). James wrote a speech to present to his class, telling his peers that people with Asperger's think differently and sometimes have difficulty understanding things. He reflected that sometimes teachers expected him just to "get on with it" in class, but he was not like other students and sometimes needed more help. He said that he wanted to be on the SRC so he could help other students with Asperger's at the school by talking to the teachers and teaching them about Asperger's. That way he could help make the school great for everybody. James was very proud of himself for giving his speech, as were his parents; and his peers must have been impressed too because he was elected to the SRC.

Chapter 15

TROUBLESHOOTING

Just as many parents have concerns about telling their child they have autism, concerns are often raised by parents about how others will react when told about a child's diagnosis.

Whether you are telling others in order to arrange accommodations and support for your child, or to encourage understanding and acceptance, the reactions of the people in your child's life can vary greatly, from offers of assistance and guidance, to denial and rejection.

Thankfully, most people whom you speak to about your child's autism will react in a positive and helpful way, but it is good to be prepared for situations that may not go as planned. The following questions and discussions reflect concerns that are commonly raised by parents as they begin to share their child's diagnosis with others.

What if my family or friends make unhelpful comments or suggestions?

Sometimes family members and friends, when they are told about a child's diagnosis, seem to continually minimize a child's difficulties. I think this is more often a way for them to try to reduce a parent's distress, rather than questioning the diagnosis. However, as a parent it can feel like you are being undermined or your feelings and the seriousness of the situation are not being acknowledged.

Comments such as "He will grow out of it," "Boys are always slow to talk," "She's fine, you just need to be more firm," or "It must have been something you did when you were pregnant," can be hurtful and seem dismissive or insensitive, particularly when you may be experiencing strong emotions and may have your own doubts and concerns about the diagnosis. Unfortunately, when receiving difficult news, and being uncertain of how to respond, people often make comments that seem to dismiss a parent's concerns and minimize a child's difficulties in a misguided attempt to try to make everyone feel better.

When faced with unhelpful comments, it can be difficult not to let them upset you. However, it is important to consider what the person is trying to achieve by what they say. If the comment comes from a place of concern and caring, then it can be helpful to acknowledge the person's concern, but let them know that you don't need them to try to make you feel better. What you need instead is for them to listen and understand what you are going through, and be there to support you when you need it. In contrast, if the comment seems to come from a place of ignorance or denial, you may want to try to educate the person about autism and help them understand your child and their particular needs.

Occasionally, despite providing information and letting a friend or family member know what you need from them, some people will continue to be unhelpful in their comments and attitude toward your child's diagnosis. When this occurs, you may need to consider creating some distance between yourself and the person in question, to protect yourself from their negative influence. If distance is not possible, you may want to adapt your relationship with the person so that discussion regarding your child and autism can be limited or avoided.

In these situations, it is also important to remember that while others may have different opinions and levels of understanding regarding your child's diagnosis, you are the expert on your child and their needs. You can have confidence in your path to the point of diagnosis, and the professionals who have assisted you along the way. What family and friends say about your child's diagnosis does not change that.

What if my partner does not want to share our child's diagnosis?

Sharing a child's autism diagnosis is a big step in the journey of a parent. As we discussed earlier, parents experience their journey in different ways, and as such may have different ideas about when they should share their child's diagnosis and with whom.

If you find yourself in a situation where you are ready to share your child's diagnosis but your partner is not, it can cause a great deal of conflict and discord within your relationship. It is important in this situation to communicate clearly about your reasons for sharing your child's diagnosis, and what telling others about your child's autism will achieve, and also to listen to and acknowledge your partner's concerns.

I find that the most effective way of managing this difference of opinion is to discuss who it might be essential to tell, or who both of you feel would be the most important person to tell. If you can decide together on one trusted person to share the diagnosis with at first, this will then help pave the way for other people to be informed once your partner sees the benefits of telling others about your child's needs and experiences a positive reaction to sharing your child's diagnosis.

What if my child's teacher thinks they know everything about autism and won't look at my child's individual needs?

Every now and then, I come across a teacher or carer who seems very confident in their knowledge of autism and how to support autistic children, but who is resistant to learning about any new interventions or tailoring things specifically to an individual child's needs.

Obviously, having knowledge and experience in working with children with autism is fantastic. However, all children with autism have their own personalities and different levels of need, and a 'one size fits all' approach does not work. Further, autism is commonly accompanied by any of a range of other difficulties including anxiety, dyspraxia, attention deficit hyperactivity disorder (ADHD) and learning difficulties, and the addition of one or more of these disorders can dramatically change a child's presentation and the strategies that need to be introduced to support them.

If a teacher or carer is resistant to taking on new strategies to support your child, talk to them about your child's specific needs and how the suggested strategies will support them. Using practical examples of your child's difficulties in an area and the difference that a strategy can make to support them can also be useful. It can also be helpful to enlist the support of one of your child's therapists to suggest and reinforce the best ways to help your child, by providing a list of recommendations or meeting with the teacher to discuss your child and further explain why specific interventions are necessary.

What if my family and friends will not accept my child's diagnosis for cultural or religious reasons?

For many families with diverse backgrounds, talking about a child's diagnosis involves the added complication of considering how autism, and often disability in general, is viewed by family and friends with strong cultural and religious beliefs.

When having a child with autism is viewed by members of your community as a punishment for past indiscretions, or a shameful secret that should not be acknowledged or discussed, it can be extremely isolating and upsetting. Parents are often left feeling that they are unable to share their child's diagnosis with those closest to them, for fear of judgment and exclusion. While some information may be able to be safely disclosed, such as a child having some difficulties with talking or learning, it may be that autism itself cannot be mentioned, creating a situation in which parents cannot be fully open and honest with their usual support network.

In these situations, I think it is extremely important for parents to seek out people and services that can support them outside of their community, to ensure they have the opportunity to be open and honest about their challenges and receive the help and understanding that they need. Some families whom I work with have found that talking to other parents of children with autism at their child's early intervention service or school, or connecting with parents through autism support groups, also helps them to feel supported and understood.

In this way, these parents can maintain important relationships in their lives within their community, and also receive the support that is essential to their wellbeing and their autistic child's progress.

PART 3

RESOURCES

Chapter 16

DOWNLOADABLE WORKSHEETS

The following pages have been designed to assist you to talk to your child about their autism diagnosis, and also to provide information about your child to teachers and carers. Examples of what each sheet will look like once completed have also been included for your information.

ARE WE SIMILAR OR DIFFERENT?

Think about a friend or family
member that you are close to.

What have you noticed that you have in
common? What is different about each of you?

Use the boxes below to list how you and your
friend/family member are similar and different.

What do I have in common with _____?

How are we the same?

How are we different?

What is good about being similar to others?

_____

What is good about being different from others?

_____

ARE WE SIMILAR OR DIFFERENT?

Think about a friend or family member that you are close to.

What have you noticed that you have in common? What is different about each of you?

Use the boxes below to list how you and your friend/family member are similar and different.

What do I have in common with ____Thomas____?

How are we the same?

We have brown hair

We go to the same school

We play basketball

We like eating peanut butter

We both have a sister

We love playing computer games

How are we different?

Thomas has blue eyes, mine are green

I am taller than Thomas

Thomas does karate

I have autism

I love trains, Thomas doesn't

What is good about being similar to others?

We have things we like to do together and talk about.

What is good about being different from others?

We can come up with different ideas for playing.

WHAT ARE MY STRENGTHS AND CHALLENGES?

When we think about our abilities, we all have things that we do well (strengths) and things we need help with (challenges). In the boxes below, make a list of some things you do well and some things you need help with.

Things I do well	Things I need help with

Now, think about how you can use the things you are good at to help with the things you struggle with. Draw a line between the strengths and challenges that could go together.

WHAT ARE MY STRENGTHS AND CHALLENGES?

When we think about our abilities, we all have things that we do well (strengths) and things we need help with (challenges). In the boxes below, make a list of some things you do well and some things you need help with.

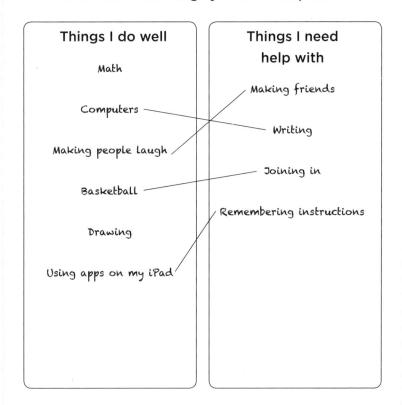

Now, think about how you can use the things you are good at to help with the things you struggle with. Draw a line between the strengths and challenges that could go together.

WHAT ARE MY INGREDIENTS?

There are many different qualities that go together to make you who you are, and autism or Asperger's is just one of them. On the page below, put your name in the space at the top, then add all your ingredients or qualities around the picture.

WHAT ARE MY INGREDIENTS?

There are many different qualities that go together to make you who you are, and autism or Asperger's is just one of them. On the page below, put your name in the space at the top, then add all your ingredients or qualities around the picture.

WHAT ARE MY INGREDIENTS?

There are many different qualities that go together to make you who you are, and autism or Asperger's is just one of them. On the page below, put your name in the space at the top, then add all your ingredients or qualities around the picture.

Sophie

Clever

Bendy

Caring

Patient

Brave

Kind

Asperger's

Funny

HOW IS AUTISM LIKE A STEAM ENGINE?

Steam engines and diesels are both useful and powerful trains but they work slightly differently. They both have things they do well and things that are harder for them.

Steam engines need wood and water to power their engine, but diesel engines need diesel fuel to run.

Steam engines are better suited to moving carriages, while diesel engines are better for moving heavy cargo.

When a steam engine needs to move cargo, it might need to work harder, but it can still get the job done.

Having autism means your brain works differently compared to children who don't have autism.

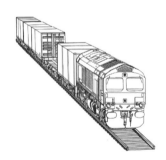

Sometimes you might have to work harder than other children to get a job done, just like the steam engine, but you can still do it if you try.

Having autism means you are different, but being different is not good or bad, it is just different.

HELP THE CAR AND THE BUS GET TO SCHOOL

Take the car on the shortest route to school. Use a blue pencil to mark the way. With a red pencil, mark the route the bus takes to school. Make sure it goes to all the bus stops along the way.

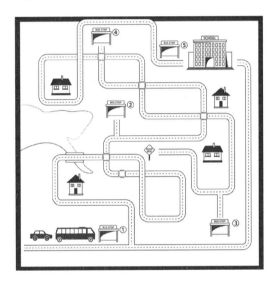

Both the bus and the car will get children to school, but the bus takes longer because it makes a lot of stops on the way.

Just like the bus takes longer than the car to get to school, sometimes children with autism take longer to do things than other children because their brain works in a different way.

Taking longer does not mean you can't do something, it just means you do it differently.

LAPTOP VS TABLET - IS ONE BETTER THAN THE OTHER OR ARE THEY JUST DIFFERENT?

Laptops and tablets have different operating systems that enable them to work effectively, but they are able to complete most of the same functions.

On the lines below, list as many similarities between laptops and tablets as you can.

_____

_____

_____

Just like laptops and tablets, people with autism and people without autism have different operating systems – their brains.

Even though their brains work differently, people with autism can do the same things that other people can do.

Having autism does not make a person more or less skilled than others, it just makes them different.

LAPTOP VS TABLET - IS ONE BETTER THAN THE OTHER OR ARE THEY JUST DIFFERENT?

Laptops and tablets have different operating systems that enable them to work effectively, but they are able to complete most of the same functions.

On the lines below, list as many similarities between laptops and tablets as you can.

You can take them with you wherever you go.

They need electricity to work.

You can play games on them. You can write stories on them.

Just like laptops and tablets, people with autism and people without autism have different operating systems – their brains.

Even though their brains work differently, people with autism can do the same things that other people can do.

Having autism does not make a person more or less skilled than others, it just makes them different.

ALL ABOUT ME

My name is _____.
I have autism.

The most important thing
to know about me is:

_____

_____

_____

I am good at:

_____

_____

_____

I like:

_____

_____

_____

I don't like:

_____

_____

_____

I need help with:

_____

_____

_____

You can help me by:

_____

_____

_____

Things that can upset me are:

_____

_____

_____

When I get upset I:

_____

_____

_____

You can help me by:

_____

_____

_____

ALL ABOUT ME

My name is _Molly_ .
I have autism.

**The most important thing
to know about me is:**

I am very social and it is important that I feel a

sense of connection with my peers. At times, I can

misunderstand social cues and can be extremely sensitive.

I am good at:

I have a very vivid and detailed imagination.

My singing voice is lovely and strong! I have a

brilliant memory and am a gifted mimic.

I like:

Music, singing, dancing, storytelling and play

acting. The Wiggles, Peppa Pig and many a musical:

Annie, Wizard of Oz, Willy Wonka, etc.

I don't like:

'Bad dreams!' I become so caught up inside my story I

have trouble distinguishing between fantasy and reality.

I need help with:

Understanding the thoughts, feelings and
intentions of others. Managing and validating my
(confusing!) emotions and those of others.

You can help me by:

Explaining social contexts when I seem
confused or misinterpret situations, then
validating my feelings in a soft manner.

Things that can upset me are:

I am highly intuitive to people's moods and emotions,
especially if they are angry. Sometimes laughter, if
I think the laughter is being directed at me.

When I get upset I:

I will often show my fear and anger by using inappropriate language
and tone of voice and am locked tight on 'repeat cycle.' I can run,
hide, attempt escape – particularly if I feel very threatened and scared.

You can help me by:

Providing a 'safe zone' – a quiet, local, private space
I can withdraw to, especially in a heightened state of
distress. Giving me a gentle back rub or tickle.

ALL ABOUT ME

My name is _____.
I have autism.

The most important thing
to know about me is:

I am good at:

I like:

I don't like:

I need help with:

You can help me by:

Things that can upset me are:

When I get upset I:

You can help me by:

ALL ABOUT ME

My name is ___Tom_____.
I have autism.

The most important thing to know about me is:

I have a great sense of humor and I really like to help. Sometimes it is hard for me to make good choices about my behavior but I am trying hard to improve.

I am good at:

Math, basketball, using the computer, making people laugh

I like:

Sport, dinosaurs, math, Minecraft

I don't like:

Loud noises, people sitting too close to me, writing, sad music

I need help with:

- Understanding my friends' thoughts and feelings, especially in the playground
- Writing stories

You can help me by:

- Explaining social situations as they are happening
- Talking through some ideas with me before I start writing

Things that can upset me are:

- Changes in my routine
- Not understanding what to do
- Crowds of people and loud noises
- People not following the rules

When I get upset I:

- Raise my voice and yell
- Pace around the room
- Hit out at people close to me
- Destroy my work

You can help me by:

- Giving me frequent breaks from the classroom
- Setting up a quiet space for me to go to so I can calm down

Chapter 17

HELPFUL BOOKS, VIDEOS AND WEBSITES

Books

BOOKS FOR CHILDREN WITH AUTISM

The ASD and Me Picture Book: A Visual Guide to Understanding Challenges and Strengths for Children on the Autism Spectrum by Joel Shaul. London: Jessica Kingsley Publishers, 2017.

I Am an Aspie Girl: A Book for Young Girls with Autism Spectrum Conditions by Danuta Bulhak-Paterson. London: Jessica Kingsley Publishers, 2015.

My Autism Book: A Child's Guide to Their Autism Spectrum Diagnosis by Glòria Durà-Vilà and Tamar Levi. London: Jessica Kingsley Publishers, 2014.

A Special Book about Me: A Book for Children Diagnosed with Asperger Syndrome by Josie Santomauro. London: Jessica Kingsley Publishers, 2009.

All My Stripes: A Story for Children with Autism by Shaina Rudolph and Danielle Royer. Washington, DC: Magination Press, 2015.

The Survival Guide for Kids with Autism Spectrum Disorders (And Their Parents) by Elizabeth Verdick and Elizabeth Reeve. Surry Hills, NSW: Read How You Want, 2015.

Me and My Brain: Ellie's Story by Antoniette Preston and Kerryn Lisa. Bacchus Marsh, Vic: Sister Sensory, 2017.

Me and My Brain: Ethan's Story by Antoniette Preston and Kerryn Lisa. Bacchus Marsh, Vic: Sister Sensory, 2017.

I Am Utterly Unique: Celebrating the Strengths of Children with Aspergers Syndrome and High-Functioning Autism by Elaine Marie Larson. Lenexa KS: AAPC, 2006.

The Asperger Children's Toolkit by Francis Musgrave. London: Jessica Kingsley Publishers, 2012.

BOOKS FOR ADOLESCENTS WITH AUTISM

The Asperkid's (Secret) Book of Social Rules: The Handbook of Not-So-Obvious Social Guidelines for Tweens and Teens with Asperger Syndrome by Jennifer Cook O'Toole. London: Jessica Kingsley Publishers, 2012.

Different Like Me: My Book of Autism Heroes by Jennifer Elder. London: Jessica Kingsley Publishers, 2006.

Freaks, Geeks and Asperger Syndrome: A User Guide to Adolescence by Luke Jackson. London: Jessica Kingsley Publishers, 2002.

BOOKS TO HELP CHILDREN UNDERSTAND AUTISM

A Girl Like Tilly: Growing Up with Autism by Helen Bates and Ellen Li. London: Jessica Kingsley Publishers, 2016.

Why Johnny Doesn't Flap: NT Is OK! by Clay Morton and Gail Morton. London: Jessica Kingsley Publishers, 2015.

Inside Asperger's Looking Out by Kathy Hoopmann. London: Jessica Kingsley Publishers, 2012.

Kevin Thinks…about Outer Space, Confusing Expressions and the Perfectly Logical World of Asperger Syndrome by Gail Watts. London: Jessica Kingsley Publishers, 2012.

Brotherly Feelings: Me, My Emotions, and My Brother with Asperger's Syndrome by Sam Frender and Robin Schiffmiller. London: Jessica Kingsley Publishers, 2007.

All Cats Have Asperger Syndrome by Kathy Hoopmann. London: Jessica Kingsley Publishers, 2006.

Since We're Friends: An Autism Picture Book by Celeste Shally. New York, NY: Sky Pony Press, 2012.

My Brother Charlie by Holly Robinson Peete and Ryan Elizabeth Peete. New York, NY: Scholastic Press, 2010.

The Autism Acceptance Book: Being a Friend to Someone with Autism by Ellen Sabin. New York, NY: Watering Can Press, 2008.

Autism, the Invisible Cord: A Sibling's Diary by Barbara S. Cain. Washington, DC: Magination Press, 2012.

Everybody Is Different: A Book for Young People Who Have Brothers or Sisters with Autism by Fiona Bleach. London: National Autistic Society, 2001.

Leah's Voice by Lori Demonia. San Antonio, TX: Halo Publishing International, 2012.

Spaghetti Is Not a Finger Food and Other Life Lessons by Jodi Carmichael. Belvedere, CA: Little Pickle Press LLC, 2013.

All about My Brother by Sarah Peralta. Lenexa, KS: AAPC Publishing, 2002.

What It Is to Be Me! An Asperger Kid Book by Angela Wine. *Fairdale, KY: Fairdale Publishing, 2005.*

Why Does Izzy Cover Her Ears? Dealing with Sensory Overload by Jennifer Veenendall. Shawnee Mission, KS: AAPC, 2009.

Tacos Anyone? by Marvie Ellis. Round Rock, TX: Speech Kids Texas Press Inc., 2005.

A is for Autism, F is for Friend: A Kid's Book for Making Friends with a Child Who Has Autism by Joanna Keating-Velasco. Shawnee Mission, KS: AAPC Publishing, 2007.

Do You Understand Me? My Life, My Thoughts, My Autism Spectrum Disorder by Sofie Koborg Brøsen. London: Jessica Kingsley Publishers, 2006.

BOOKS TO HELP FAMILY AND FRIENDS UNDERSTAND AUTISM

Can I tell you about Autism? A guide for friends, family and professionals by Jude Welton. London: Jessica Kingsley Publishers, 2014.

Can I tell you about Asperger Syndrome? A guide for friends and family by Jude Welton. London: Jessica Kingsley Publishers, 2003.

Understanding Autism for Dummies by Stephen Shore and Linda G. Rastelli. Indianapolis, IN: Wiley, 2006.

The Complete Guide to Asperger's Syndrome by Tony Attwood. London: Jessica Kingsley Publishers, 2008.

What Is It Like to Be Me? A Book about a Boy with Asperger's Syndrome by Alenka Klemenc. London: Jessica Kingsley Publishers, 2013.

Adolescents on the Autism Spectrum: A Parent's Guide to the Cognitive, Social, Physical, and Transition Needs of Teenagers with Autism Spectrum Disorders by Chantal Sicile-Kira and Temple Grandin. London: Vermilion, 2007.

Aspergirls: Empowering Females with Asperger Syndrome by Rudy Simone. London: Jessica Kingsley Publishers, 2010.

Pretending to Be Normal: Living with Asperger's Syndrome by Liane Holliday Willey. London: Jessica Kingsley Publishers, 1999.

Videos

VIDEOS FOR CHILDREN AND ADOLESCENTS ABOUT AUTISM

Amazing Things Happen
www.youtube.com/watch?v=Ezv85LMFx2E

Marvelous Max
www.youtube.com/watch?v=wc77MksM_2c

Sesame Street and Autism: We're Amazing, 1, 2, 3!
www.youtube.com/watch?v=fI-Sk7_ykzU

Sesame Street: Meet Julia (Full Clip | 10 Min)
www.youtube.com/watch?v=dKCdV20zLMs

My Autism and Me
www.youtube.com/watch?v=ejpWWP1HNGQ

Rosie King: How Autism Freed Me to Be Myself
www.youtube.com/watch?v=jQ95xlZeHo8

Arthur – When Carl Met George
https://pbskids.org/video/arthur/1447843659

A is for Autism, F is for Friend
www.youtube.com/watch?v=bbnppZp6jxA

VIDEOS FOR FAMILY AND FRIENDS ABOUT AUTISM

Rosie King: How Autism Freed Me to Be Myself
www.youtube.com/watch?v=jQ95xlZeHo8

Steve Silberman: The Forgotten History of Autism
www.youtube.com/watch?v=_MBiP3G2Pzc

Autism – How My Unstoppable Mother Proved the Experts Wrong: Chris Varney at TEDxMelbourne
www.youtube.com/watch?v=T1HQKB2txgY

Living with Autism – Ky's Story
www.youtube.com/watch?v=p4J59GY8DR4

Stephen Shore – Should You Tell Your Child about His/Her Autism Diagnosis?
www.youtube.com/watch?v=MmrR4UgKFyA

Useful websites

The National Autistic Society
www.autism.org.uk

American Autism Association
www.myautism.org

Autism Speaks
www.autismspeaks.org

Amaze
www.amaze.org.au

Aspect
www.autismspectrum.org.au

BIBLIOGRAPHY

Cadogan, S. (2015) 'Parent Reported Impacts of Their Disclosure of Their Child's ASD Diagnosis to Their Children.' Calgary: University of Calgary. Accessed on 10/06/17 at http://theses.ucalgary.ca/handle/11023/2298

Coburn-Snyder, H. (2012) *School Community Tool Kit.* Autism Speaks. Accessed on 10/06/17 at www.autismspeaks.org/family-services/tool-kits/school-community-tool-kit

Elichaoff, F. (2015) 'What's it like being you? Growing old(er) with autism spectrum conditions – a scoping study.' *The European Journal of Social and Behavioural Sciences 13,* 1851–64.

Fodden, T. and Anderson, C. (2014) *ASD diagnosis: What do we tell the kids?* Interactive Autism Network. Accessed on 12/10/16 at https://iancommunity.org/cs/articles/telling_a_child_about_his_asd

Glasberg, B.A. (2000) 'The development of siblings' understanding of autism spectrum disorders.' *Journal of Autism and Developmental Disorders 30,* 2, 143–56.

I Am Cadence (2016) 'What are your ingredients?' 'I Am Cadence' Facebook page. Accessed on 10/06/17 at www.facebook.com/1032108113468280/photos/a.1034007243278367.1073741829.1032108113468280/121819 2274859862/?type=3&theater

Jarrett, H. (2014) 'An exploration of identity formation in autistic adolescents, its relationship with psychological wellbeing, and the role of mainstream education provision in the identity formation process.' University of Exeter. Accessed on 10/06/17 at https://ore.exeter.ac.uk/repository/handle/10871/15770

Jones, L., Goddard. L., Hill, E., Henry, L. and Crane, L. (2014) 'Experiences of receiving a diagnosis of autism spectrum disorder: A survey of adults in the United Kingdom.' *Journal of Autism and Developmental Disorders 44*, 3033–44.

Kerr, K. (2011) *Sharing the diagnosis of Autism Spectrum Disorder.* Accessed on 10/06/17 at www.amaze.org.au/uploads/2011/08/Fact-Sheet-Sharing-the-Diagnosis-of-Autism-Spectrum-Disorder-Aug-20111.pdf

National Autistic Society (2016) *After your child's diagnosis.* Accessed on 10/06/17 at www.autism.org.uk/about/diagnosis/children/recently-diagnosed.aspx

Santomauro, J. (1999) *When and how to tell your child they are on the Autism Spectrum.* Accessed on 10/06/17 at www.autism-help.org/family-telling-your-child.htm

Shore, S. (2010) *Should you tell your child about his/her autism diagnosis?* Accessed on 10/06/17 at www.youtube.com/watch?v=MmrR4UgKFyA

Ward, E. (2014) 'Parental accounts of sharing an autism spectrum diagnosis with their child – a thematic analysis.' University of Nottingham. Accessed on 10/06/17 at http://eprints.nottingham.ac.uk/27729

Wheeler, M. (2003) 'Getting started: Introducing your child to his or her diagnosis of autism or Asperger syndrome.' *The Reporter 9*, 1, 1–5. Accessed on 10/06/17 at www.iidc.indiana.edu/index.php?pageId=362

INDEX